Maria Parloa

The Appledore cook book

Containing practical receipts for plain and rich cooking

Maria Parloa

The Appledore cook book
Containing practical receipts for plain and rich cooking

ISBN/EAN: 9783744785945

Printed in Europe, USA, Canada, Australia, Japan

Cover: Foto ©Lupo / pixelio.de

More available books at **www.hansebooks.com**

THE
APPLEDORE COOK BOOK

CONTAINING

Practical Receipts

FOR

PLAIN AND RICH COOKERY

By M^{rs}. PARLOA.

NEW EDITION.

BOSTON:
ANDREW F. GRAVES,
1880.

Entered, according to

By M

In the Office of the Libr

PREFACE.

In ▓▓▓▓▓ little book to the public, I am aware ▓▓▓▓▓ many good cook books in the market ▓▓▓▓▓ ut I trust that this will supply a want ▓▓▓▓▓ lways been felt by young housekeepers ▓▓▓▓▓ trouble with all the cook books which ▓▓▓▓▓ n (and I am constantly hearing the sa▓▓▓▓▓ t) is, that they are too expensive, a▓▓▓▓▓ use weight instead of measure, and al▓▓▓▓▓ take for granted that the young housek▓▓▓▓▓ many things which she really does n▓▓▓▓▓ t I have endeavored to supply in this ▓▓▓▓▓. Having had years of experience a▓▓▓▓▓ ivate families and hotels, I know the wa▓▓▓▓▓ sses, and feel competent to supply th▓▓▓▓▓

I ha▓▓▓▓▓ this book in two parts — one for plain, ▓▓▓▓▓ ich cooking. In the First Part will be found minute directions for cooking everything that is within the reach of an ordinary family. In Part Second will be found directions for richer cooking. There is not one receipt in the book which has not been *proved* to be good. There are very few which I have not used myself, and of the value of those I am fully assured, having seen nearly all of them tried. The rules for jellies, charlotte russe, and creams will be found to be worth twice the price of the book. Many of the visitors to the Rockingham House, Portsmouth, N. H., Pavilion Hotel, Wolfborough, N. H., McMillan House, North Conway, N. H., and the Appledore House, Isle of Shoals, will find many dishes with which they expressed themselves pleased while the writer was pastry cook at those houses.

PREFACE TO SECOND EDITION.

FIVE years have passed since the first edition of The Appledore Cook Book was given to the public; and, in that time, the author has been adding to her store of *tried* receipts, and now feels it a duty and a pleasure to give them to the public.

The Appendix will be found to have been written on the first plan of the book; that is, that there was to be nothing inserted which was not *tried* and *practical*.

MANDARIN, FLA., APRIL 6, 1877.

ns.

CONTENTS.

PART FIRST.

	PAGE		
Fish Ch...	17	Stewed Lobster,	
Fish Ch...	18	Curried Lobster,	
Clam Cl...	18	Eels, Fried,	
Clam Cl...	19	Baked Eels,	
Boiled C...	19	Remarks in regard to Fish,	
Fried C...	20		
Broiled...	20	**SOUP.**	
Baked C...	21		
Tongue...	21	Beef Soup,	
Salt Cod...	22	Mutton Broth,	
Broiled...	23	Mutton Broth, No. 2,	
Salt Fis...	23	Dumplings for Soup,	
Fish Ba...	23	Veal Soup,	
Another...	24	Pea Soup,	
Another...	24		
Fish H...	24		
Boiled...	25	**MEATS.**	
Fried...	25		
Broiled...	25	Boiled Corned Beef,	
Smoke...	26	Boiled Salt Tongue,	
Boiled...	26	Boiled Fresh Tongue,	
Fried...	26	Boiled Flank of Beef,	
Broiled...	26	Boiled Ham,	
Salmon...	26	Boiled Leg of Mutton,	
Shad a...	26	Boiled Shoulder of Mutton,	
Fresh ...od,	26	Boiled Leg or Shoulder of Lamb,	
Broiled...	27		
Fried...	27	Boiled Fowl and Pork	
Baked...	27	Boiled Veal,	
To Br... Mackerel,	27	Boiled Turkey,	
Salt M... n,	28	Roast Beef,	
To Bo...	28	Roast Mutton,	
Smelts...	28	Roast Lamb,	
Brook...	28	Roast Veal,	
To Bo...	29	Roast Pork,	

CONTENTS.

	PAGE		PAGE
Broiled Beefsteak,	43	Boiled Sweet Potatoes,	62
Fried Beefsteak,	44	Baked Sweet Potatoes,	62
Beefsteak Smothered in Onions,	44	Boiled Onions,	62
Italianed Beef,	45	Fried Onions,	63
Stewed Beef,	45	Boiled Squash,	63
Fricassee of Beef,	46	Baked Squash,	63
Mutton Chops,	46	Beets,	64
Mutton Pie with Tomatoes,	46	Pickled Beets,	64
Mutton Pie, Plain,	46	Shelled Beans,	64
Mutton Fricassee,	47	Baked Beans,	64
Haricot of Mutton,	47	String Beans,	65
Minced Mutton,	47	Stewed Beans,	65
Lamb Chops,	48	Green Peas,	65
Broiled Veal,	48	Green Corn,	66
Fricassee of Veal,	48	Boiled Turnips,	66
Veal Cutlets,	49	Boiled Parsnips,	66
Veal on Toast,	49	Fried Parsnips,	66
Veal Croquettes,	49	Boiled Carrots,	67
Pork Steak,	50	Boiled Rice,	67
Fried Salt Pork,	50	Another Mode,	67
Broiled Salt Pork,	50	Stewed Tomatoes,	68
Salt Pork Fried in Batter,	50	Sliced Tomatoes,	68
Fried Sausages,	51	Baked Tomatoes,	68
Broiled Sausages,	51	Asparagus,	69
Pigs' Feet, Soused,	51	Spinage,	69
Fried Pigs' Feet,	52	Cabbage,	69
Pigs' Feet, Fried in Batter,	52	Cauliflower,	70
Pigs' Head Cheese,	52	Dandelions,	70
Fried Ham,	53	Beet Greens,	70
Broiled Ham,	53	Macaroni, Boiled,	71
Ham and Eggs,	53		
Fried Liver,	54		
Broiled Liver,	54	**BREAD.**	
Boiled Tripe,	54		
Broiled Tripe,	54	Hop Yeast,	73
Fried Tripe,	55	Hop Yeast, No. 2,	73
Soused Tripe,	55	Potato Yeast,	74
Tripe Fried in Batter,	55	Yeast Bread,	74
Calf's Head and Pluck,	55	Yeast Bread, No. 2,	75
Hash made from Calf's Head and Pluck,	56	Milk Yeast Bread,	76
Meat Hash,	56	Graham Bread,	77
		Third Bread,	77
		Brown Bread,	77
		Brown Bread, No. 2,	78
VEGETABLES.		Brown Bread, No. 3,	78
		Raised Biscuit,	78
Boiled Potatoes,	59	Raised Biscuit, No. 2,	79
Mashed Potatoes,	59	White Mountain Rolls,	80
Browned Potatoes,	60	Parker House Rolls,	80
Baked Potatoes,	60	Coffee Rolls,	80
Fried Potatoes,	60	Buns,	81
Fried Boiled Potatoes,	61	Soda Biscuit,	81
Potatoes warmed with Pork,	61	Cream of Tartar Rolls,	81
Potatoes warmed in Gravy,	62	Sour Milk Biscuit,	82
Fricassee of Potatoes,	62	Buttermilk Rolls,	82

CONTENTS.

	PAGE
Graham Rolls,	82
Graham Rolls, No. 2,	83
Corn Rolls,	83
Corn Cake,	83
Corn Cake, No. 2,	83
Corn Cake, No. 3,	84
Corn Cake, No. 4,	84
Rye Drop Cakes,	84
Flour Drop Cakes,	85
Flour Drop Cakes, No. 2,	85
Graham Drop Cakes,	85
Muffins,	85
Muffins, No. 2,	86
Griddle Cakes,	86
Rice Cakes,	86
Indian Cakes,	86
Corn Dodgers,	87
Bread Cakes,	87
Buckwheat Cakes,	87
Fried Mush,	88
Brown Bread Brewis,	88

PLAIN CAKE.

Tea Cake,	89
Berry Cake,	89
Plain Cup Cake,	89
Richer Cup Cake,	90
Railroad Cake,	90
Cream Cake,	90
Feather Cake,	91
Sponge Cake,	91
Sponge Cake, No. 2,	91
Allie's Cake,	92
Raisin Cake,	92
Apple Cake,	92
Rich Molasses Gingerbread,	93
Soft Molasses Gingerbread, No. 2,	93
Soft Molasses Gingerbread, No. 3,	93
Hard Molasses Gingerbread,	94
Hard Sugar Gingerbread,	94
Ginger Snaps,	94
Molasses Cookies,	95
Vinegar Cookies,	95
Sugar Cookies,	95
Jumbles,	96
Plain Doughnuts,	96
Raised Doughnuts,	97

PUDDINGS.

	PAGE
Boiled Rice,	98
Boiled Rice, No. 2,	98
Baked Rice,	98
Baked Rice, No. 2,	99
Minute Pudding,	99
Corn Starch Pudding,	100
Quaking Pudding,	100
Bride's Pudding,	101
Bread Pudding,	101
Whortleberry Pudding,	101
Plain Whortleberry Pudding,	102
Boiled Apple Pudding,	102
Boiled Batter Pudding,	103
Baked Apple Pudding,	104
Pan Dowdy,	104
Apple Dowdy,	104
Apple Charlotte,	105
Apple and Sago Pudding,	105
Tapioca and Apple Pudding,	106
Boiled Tapioca Pudding,	106
Baked Tapioca Pudding,	106
Custard Pudding,	107
Baked Indian Pudding,	107
Cottage Pudding,	107
Sponge Pudding,	108
Italian Fritters,	108

PIES.

Plain Pie Crust,	109
Cream Paste,	109
Sliced Apple Pies,	110
Stewed Apple Pies,	110
Dried Apple Pies,	110
Berry Pies,	111
Rhubarb Pies,	111
Squash Pies,	111
Cranberry Pies,	112
Gooseberry Pies,	112
Pumpkin Pies,	112
Custard Pies,	112
Mince Pies,	113
Mock Mince Pies,	113
Lemon Pies,	114
Cream Pies,	114
Filling for Cream Pies,	114
Washington Pies,	115
Remarks,	115

PART SECOND.

SOUPS.

	PAGE
Soup Stock,	117
Brown Soup,	118
Brown Soup, No. 2,	119
Brown Soup, No. 3,	119
Vegetable Soup,	119
Julienne Soup,	120
Barley Soup,	120
Sago Soup,	120
Macaroni Soup,	120
Vermicilli Soup,	120
Ox-tail Soup,	121
Tomato Soup,	121
Giblet Soup,	121
Turkey Soup,	121
Chicken Soup,	122
White Soup,	122
Beef Soup,	122
Mock Turtle Soup,	123
Oyster Soup,	124

FISH.

Baked Cod or Salmon,	125
Scalloped Fish,	125

POULTRY.

To clean Poultry,	126
Roast Turkey,	126
Roast Chicken,	127
Roast Goose,	128
Roast Duck,	128
Roast Partridges,	128
Roast Grouse,	129
Roast Pigeons,	129
Small Birds,	129

VENISON.

Roast Venison,	130

ENTREMETS.

Stewed Beef, with Mushrooms,	131
Fillet of Beef, with Mushrooms,	131
Alamode Beef,	131

	PAGE
Boulli Beef,	132
Boulli Tongue,	133
Stewed Partridges,	133
Brown Fricassee of Chicken,	133
White Fricassee of Chicken,	134
Chicken Curry,	134
Chicken Pie,	134
Salad Dressing,	134
Broiled Chicken,	135
Chicken Salad,	135
Lobster Salad,	135
Chicken Patties,	135
Deviled Turkey,	136
Potted Pigeon,	136
Pigeon Pie,	136
Quail Pie,	137
Snipe Pie,	137
Oyster Pie,	137
Oyster Patties,	137
Oyster Roast,	137
Scalloped Oysters,	138
Fried Oysters,	138
Broiled Oysters,	138
Veal Croquettes,	138
Rice Croquettes,	139
Macaroni in Cream,	139
Queen Fritters,	139
Plain Fritters,	140
Apple Fritters,	140
Pancakes,	140

PUDDINGS.

Baltimore Pudding,	141
Wedding Pudding,	141
Plum Pudding,	142
Christmas Pudding,	142
Bread and Butter Pudding,	142
Snow Pudding,	143
Sauce for Snow Pudding,	143
Cocoanut Pudding,	144
Cocoanut Pudding, No. 2,	144
Ginger Pudding,	144
Beverly Pudding,	145
Lemon Pudding,	145
Lemon Pudding, No. 2,	146
Corn Pudding,	146
Boiled Cherry Pudding,	146
Baked Whortleberry Pudding,	146
Appledore Pudding,	147

CONTENTS.

	PAGE
Bird's Nest Pudding,	147
Rice Meringue,	147
Pavilion Pudding,	148
Frozen Pudding,	148
Fruit Pudding,	143
Almond Pudding,	149
Sunderland Pudding,	149
Pineapple Pudding,	149
Omelet Souffle,	150

PIES.

Puff Paste,	151
Green Apple Pies,	152
Dried Apple Pies,	152
Peach Pies,	152
Plum Pies,	153
Mince Pies,	153
Lemon Pies,	153
Lemon Pies, No. 2,	154
Marlborough Pies,	154

PUDDING SAUCES.

Rich Wine Sauce,	155
Plain Wine Sauce,	155
Lemon Sauce,	155
Vinegar Sauce,	156

DISHES FOR THE SICK.

Beef Tea,	157
Chicken Broth,	157
Oatmeal Gruel,	157
Indian Meal Gruel,	158
Plum Porridge,	158
Corn Tea,	158
Cream Toast,	158
Wine Whey,	159
Vinegar Whey,	159
Sour Milk Whey,	159
A good Drink for the Lungs,	159
Another Drink,	159
Another Drink,	160
Lemonade,	160
Another Beef Tea,	160
Sack Posset,	160

DESSERTS.

Charlotte Russe,	161
Holland Cream,	162
Lemon Creams,	163

	PAGE
Velvet Cream,	163
Italian Cream,	163
Chocolate Cream,	163
Blanc-mange made with Gelatine,	164
Moss Blanc-mange,	164
Blanc-mange in Wine Sauce,	165
Wine Jelly,	165
Lemon Jelly,	165
Soft Custard,	166
Almond Custard,	166
Snowball Custard,	166
Chocolate Custard,	167
Coffee Custard,	167
Steamed Custards,	167
Baked Custards,	167
Floating Island,	168
Apple Snow,	168
Tipsy Parson,	168
Apple Float,	168
Trifle,	169
Wine Whips,	169
Fruit Whips,	169
Mock Sherbet,	169
Cream Cakes,	169
Sponge Drops,	170
Kisses,	170
Cocoanut Drops,	171
Cheese Cakes,	171
Tarts,	171
Directions for Freezing,	172
Ice Cream made with Cream,	173
Coffee Ice Cream,	173
Lemon Ice Cream,	173
Chocolate Ice Cream,	174
Lemon Sherbet,	174
Roman Punch,	174

CAKE.

Remarks,	175
One, Two, Three, Four Cake,	175
Rich Cup Cake,	176
Concord Cake,	176
Lemon Cake,	176
Harrison Cake,	176
Bangor Cake,	177
Bartlett Cake,	177
Down East Cake,	177
New York Cup Cake,	177
Champagne Cakes,	178
Queen Cake,	178
Loaf Cake,	178
Raisin Cake	179

CONTENTS.

	PAGE
Tumbler Cake,	178
Marble Cake,	179
Composition Cake,	179
Common Fruit Cake,	179
Delicate Cake,	180
Ice Cream Cake,	180
Crullers,	180
Fourth of July Cake,	180
Ginger Pound Cake,	181
Pound Cake,	181
Pound Cake, No. 2,	181
Wedding Cake,	181
Gold Cake,	182
Golden Cake, No. 2,	182
Silver Cake,	182
Silver Cake, No. 2,	182
Sponge Cake,	183
Sponge Cake, No. 2,	183
Berwick Sponge Cake,	183
Cocoanut Cake,	183
Orange Cake,	184
Filling for Orange Cake,	184
Chocolate Cake,	184
Chocolate Icing,	184
White Mountain Cake,	185
Angel Cake,	185
Vanilla Jumbles,	186

PRESERVES.

	PAGE
Preserved Peaches,	187
Preserved Pears,	188
Crab Apple Preserves,	188
Preserved Pineapple,	189
Preserved Citron Melon,	189
Preserved Apples,	189
Preserved Plums,	189
Preserved Cherries,	190
Preserved Quinces,	190
Raspberry Jam,	190
Barberries Preserved with Pears,	190
Barberries Preserved in Molasses,	191
Grape Marmalade,	191
Currant Jelly,	191
Currant Shrub,	192
Apple Jelly,	192
Quince Jelly,	192
To Can Berries,	193

PICKLES.

	PAGE
Pickled Cucumbers,	194
Tomato Pickles,	194
Tomato Pickles, No. 2,	195
Piccalilli,	195
Tomato Catsup,	195

SAUCES.

	PAGE
Drawn Butter,	196
Egg Sauce,	196
Oyster Sauce,	196
Celery Sauce,	196
Caper Sauce,	197
Mint Sauce,	197
Bread Sauce,	197
Coddled Apples,	197
Cranberry Sauce,	197
Apple Sauce,	198
Baked Pears,	198
Stewed Prunes,	198
Dried Apple Sauce,	198

DRINKS.

	PAGE
Tea,	200
Coffee,	200
Shells,	200
Chocolate,	201
Prepared Cocoa,	201

EGGS.

	PAGE
Boiled Eggs,	202
Fried Eggs,	202
Dropped Eggs,	202
Poached Eggs,	202
Scrabbled Eggs,	203
Omelets,	203

MISCELLANEOUS.

	PAGE
Buttered Toast,	204
Milk Toast,	204
French Toast,	204
Sandwiches,	205
Oyster Stew,	205
Corn Starch Cake,	205
Seed Cakes,	206
Strawberry Short Cake,	206
Cream Cakes,	206
Tapioca Cream,	207
Cider Cake,	207
Veal Loaf,	207
Lemon Pies,	208
Hop Yeast,	208
Baked Buckwheat Cakes,	208
Frosting,	209

CONTENTS.

	PAGE		PAGE
Frosting No. 2,	209	Spiced Currants,	210
Whitpot Pudding,	209	Chili Sauce,	210
Boiled Indian Pudding,	210	Graham Pies,	210

APPENDIX.

	PAGE		PAGE
Remarks on Digestion,	211	Cocoanut Drops,	225
		Railroad Cake,	225
		Regatta Cake,	225
MEDICINAL.		Federal Cake,	225
		Loaf Cake,	226
Unfailing Cure for Constipation (Mr. L. Scott),	214	Queen's Cake,	226
		Wedding Cake,	227
Cure No. 2,	214	Black Cake,	227
Diarrhœa, Cure No. 1,	215	Caramel Frosting,	227
Cure No. 2,	215	Glacic Cake,	228
Inflammation of the Bowels,	215	Golden Frosting,	228
Burns,	216	Chocolate Pies,	228
Neuralgia,	216	Filling for Chocolate Pies,	228
Growing-in Nails,	216	Sweet-potato Pie,	229
Nose-bleed,	217	English Plum Pudding,	229
Cure for Hoarseness,	217	Eve's Pudding,	229
		Amherst Pudding,	229
		Carrot Pudding,	230
MISCELLANEOUS.		Down-East Pudding,	230
		Sauce for Down-East Pudding,	230
Mock Bisque Soup,	218	Rachel Pudding,	230
Chicken Pillau,	218	Princess Pudding,	231
To Pickle Oysters,	219	Royal Cream,	231
Oatmeal,	219	Red Grout,	232
Hominy,	220	Cream Pudding Sauce,	232
Hominy Griddle-cakes,	220	Molasses Candy,	233
Waffles,	220	Peanut Candy,	233
Togus Bread,	221	Chocolate Candy,	233
Bread made with Yeast-cakes,	221	Vinegar Candy,	233
Cake without Eggs,	222	Mead, To Make,	234
Kneaded Plum Cake,	222	Mead, To Use,	234
Soft Gingerbread,	222	To Make Good Soap,	234
Molasses Pound-cake,	223	Black Walnut Stain,	234
Hard Gingerbread,	223	Roast Ham,	235
Jumbles,	223	Champagne Sauce,	235
Seed-cakes,	223	Vinaigrette Sauce,	235
Cookies,	224	Graham Bread,	235
Shrewsbury Cake,	224	Graham Muffins,	236
Sponge Rusk,	224	Rye Muffins,	236

	PAGE		PAGE
Sponge Drops,	237	To Make Frosted Cakes for Children,	239
Branched Peaches,	237	Chocolate Caramel,	239
Sour-Orange Preserves,	237	Molasses Candy,	240
Pickled Blueberries,	233	Vinegar Candy,	240
To Blanch Almonds,	238	Chocolate Creams,	240
Tainted Meat,	239	Molasses Candy,	240
To Clean new Stove-ware,	239		
To Restore Color to Furniture,	239		

THE APPLEDORE COOK BOOK.

PART FIRST.

FISH.

Chowder.

TAKE either a cod or haddock; skin it, loosen the skin about the head, and draw it down towards the tail, when it will peel off easily. Then run your knife down the back close to the bone, which you take out. Cut your fish in small pieces, and wash in cold water. Put the head on to boil in about two quarts of water, and boil twenty minutes. For a fish weighing six pounds, pare and slice *thin* five good sized potatoes, and one onion. Place a layer of potatoes and onion in the pot, then a layer of fish, dredge in a little salt, pepper, and flour. Keep putting in alternate layers of potatoes and fish until all is used. Use about one tablespoonful of salt, one teaspoonful of pepper, one teacup of flour, in all.

Have ready half a pound of salt pork fried brown. Pour this over the mixture; add about two quarts of cold water, then strain on the water in which the head ha been boiled. If this is not water enough to cover, add more cold. Cover tight, and boil gently thirty minutes. If not seasoned enough, add what you please. When it has boiled twenty minutes, put in six crackers which have been soaked three minutes in cold water. If you wish to add milk and butter, you can do so about five minutes before taking it up; but for my taste, it is much nicer and more natural without either.

Fish Chowder. *Mrs. T. Leighton.*

Four pounds of fish, half cod and half haddock, if you can get the two kinds, two onions, six potatoes, eight white browns, one quarter of a pound of salt pork, salt, pepper. Prepare the chowder as directed in the preceding rule; split the crackers and lay on the top, pour over the whole hot water enough to cover, and boil fifteen minutes; then wet two tablespoonfuls of flour with one third of a cup of cream. Stir this into the boiling chowder, let it boil up once, and serve. When you cannot get the white browns, pilot bread will answer. When a very strong flavor of onion is desired, use four onions.

Clam Chowder.

When intending to have clams in any form, get them in the shell if possible, the day before. Place them in a tub, and cover with clean water, and throw into this about a quart of Indian meal. This fattens them. When ready to use the clams, wash them thoroughly, then cover them with *boiling* water, and let them stand ten minutes when they will open easily. Take them from the shell, cut off the black heads, and put the bodies of the clams in a clean dish. Strain the water in which they were scalded into the kettle in which you intend to cook your chowder. To one peck of clams allow three quarts of water. Let the water come to a boil, then thicken with half a cup of flour which has been mixed with cold water, season with pepper and salt. Add the clams and a tablespoonful of butter; let it boil ten minutes. A few minutes before dishing, drop in three or four broken crackers.

Clam Chowder, No. 2.

For one peck of clams take six good-sized potatoes, pared and sliced thin, half an onion cut into pieces an inch square. Fry quarter of a pound of pork to a nice brown; place the pork and gravy, the potatoes and onions, in your kettle. Shake over the whole one tablespoonful of salt, two teaspoonfuls of pepper, and half a cup of flour. Strain over this four quarts of the water with which you scalded the clams. Place on the fire, and boil fifteen minutes, then add the clams and four split crackers; boil ten minutes longer, and serve.

Boiled Cod.

Take the head and shoulders of a good-sized cod. Scrape and wash clean; rub a handful of salt into it; flour a cloth and pin the fish in it. Put it into boiling water, and boil half an hour. Take the fish carefully from the cloth, and serve with egg sauce. Potato is the only vegetable that is nice with boiled cod.

Fried Cod.

Cut the fish into squares, wash and wipe dry. Take half a cup of flour, half a cup of sifted Indian meal, and a tablespoonful of salt. Mix all these thoroughly. Dip the fish into the mixture. Have ready a frying-pan with *boiling* fat, half lard and half pork fat; drop in your fish. Fry a dark-brown on one side, then turn and fry the same on the other side, but be very careful not to let the fish or fat burn. Have your dish hot, and lay your fish on it. Garnish the sides with the fried pork.

Broiled Cod, or Scrod.

Split, wash, and wipe dry a small cod. Rub the gridiron with a piece of fat pork, and lay the fish upon it, being careful to have the inside downward. If the fish is very thick, cook thirty minutes; but for an ordinary one, twenty minutes will be sufficient. Have the dish, in which you intend serving it, warm; place it upon the fish, and turn the dish and gridiron over simultaneously. If the fish sticks to the gridiron, loosen it gently with a knife. Have some butter warm, but *not melted*, with which to season it. Shake on a little pepper and salt and send to the table.

Baked Cod.

Scrape and wash clean a cod weighing four or five pounds. Rub into it a heaping spoonful of salt. Make a dressing of three pounded crackers, a little chopped salt pork, about one teaspoonful of parsley, a little salt and pepper, and two tablespoonfuls of cold water. Stuff the belly with this, and fasten together with a skewer. Lay thin slices of pork on the fish, which should be placed on a tin sheet that will fit loosely into the baking-pan; dredge with flour. Pour into the pan about half a pint of cold water. Baste the fish often while cooking with the water which is in the pan. If the water cooks away, add more, but do not have too much to begin with, or the fish will be boiled instead of being baked. Bake one hour. When the fish is cooked, turn the gravy into a bowl, then lift out the fish upon the tin sheet (from which you can easily slide it into the dish upon which you serve it); now turn your gravy into your baking-pan again, and place it on the fire; when it comes to a boil, thicken with a tablespoonful of flour, season with pepper and salt.

N. B. Always use a tin sheet in the baking-pan when cooking fish, as you then can preserve the shape.

Tongues and Sounds.

Soak the tongues and sounds in cold water over night. Put them in cold water and place on the fire. Let them boil thirty minutes, and serve with drawn butter.

Salt Cod Fish.

Soak a whole fish in cold water over night; in the morning wash clean, and cut off the tail and fins. If you have not a fish kettle, place it in a large milk pan, which nearly fill with water, cover, and set over a kettle of warm water. Let it cook in this way five or six hours. Serve with egg sauce and pork scraps. Potatoes, beets, and carrots are the vegetables to be served with salt fish. There are but few cooks who know how, or, if they do know, who take the pains, to get up a nice salt fish dinner; but those families who are so fortunate as to have this dish well served consider it equal to a turkey dinner; therefore I shall give minute directions for the preparation of it. One of the most essential things is to have everything *hot*. Have all your dishes warm, and dish quickly, that all may go to the table at once. Serve the fish whole; garnish the dish with a few pieces of beet and carrot. Cut your pork, and fry a nice brown. Boil an egg ten minutes, dip it into cold water, and peel of the shell. Cut it up with a silver spoon, as a knife blackens it, and put into the dish in which you intend serving the sauce. To a piece of butter the size of an egg, add a tablespoonful of flour. Blend these together well, and when the dinner is ready to serve, pour on a little less than half a pint of *boiling* water. Let this come to a boil, and pour it upon the egg. Never let drawn butter *boil*, as it becomes oily and unpalatable. The fish which is left from the dinner will be very nice for hash and fish balls.

Broiled Salt Fish.

Cut a square the size you desire, from the thickest part of the fish. Take off the skin, and wash clean; broil over clear coals ten minutes, then dip in boiling water, butter, and serve. This is a nice relish for breakfast or tea, and with boiled potatoes makes an excellent dinner.

Salt Fish in Cream.

Tear a piece of fish into small strips, wash clean, and place it in a basin with about a quart of water; let it simmer half an hour. Then pour off the water, and add one pint of new milk. When this comes to a boil, thicken with one spoonful of flour; let it boil five minutes, then add butter the size of a walnut, and a little pepper, and serve.

Fish Balls.

Take the fish left from the dinner, put it in your chopping tray, being careful that there are no bones in it; chop fine. Pare and boil potatoes enough to have twice the quantity of potatoes that you have of fish. When cooked, turn them into the tray with the fish; mash fine, and make into balls about the size of an egg. Flour the outside lightly; have the fat *boiling* hot, and fry a light brown. The fat should be half lard and half salt pork. Have the slices of pork a nice brown, and serve with the fish balls.

Another Mode.

Prepare as above; and to a quantity that will make a dozen balls add an egg, butter half the size of an egg, salt and pepper. Shape and fry as before directed.

Another Mode.

Chop fine one good sized beet, and mix well with one pint bowlful of fish and two of potato. Add to this the pork scraps left from dinner, or, if none have been left, fry a few slices of salt pork, and mix the fat with the fish and potato. Shape and fry as directed above.

Fish Hash.

Prepare the fish as for fish balls; chop fine cold potatoes, and mix with the fish. Fry brown six good slices of salt pork; take out the pork and turn the hash into the frying-pan; add half a cup of boiling water; let this heat slowly, stirring often; then spread smoothly, and brown, being careful not to let it burn. When brown, fold it as you would an omelet, dish, and garnish the dish with the slices of pork. Where pork is objected to, butter can be used instead.

Salt fish, when cooked and chopped, will keep for a week, if nothing else is mixed with it. When intending to have hash or fish balls for breakfast, the fish should be chopped the night before, and the potatoes should be pared and put in cold water. Put the potatoes on the fire as soon as it begins to burn; they will then be ready for use when you are ready for them.

Boiled Halibut.

Pour into a pan about half an inch deep of boiling water; into this lay the side of the halibut on which is the black skin; let this stand a few minutes; then scrape with a knife, when the black will be found to peel off readily. Wash clean in cold water, then pin it in your fish-cloth, and drop it into boiling water. For a piece weighing four pounds allow twenty-five minutes to boil. Serve with drawn butter.

Fried Halibut.

Take a slice of halibut, sprinkle with salt, and dredge with flour. Fry four slices of salt pork, add to the pork fat one spoonful of lard. When boiling hot put in the halibut. Fry a light brown on one side, then turn and fry the same on the other. Serve the pork with it.

Broiled Halibut.

Grease the gridiron with a little butter, place the halibut upon it, sprinkle a little salt over it, and place over clear coals. Cook one side ten minutes, then turn and cook upon the other side ten more. Have the dish warm; put the fish upon it, season with pepper and butter, and send to the table.

Smoked Halibut.

Broiled the same as the fresh, omitting the pepper and salt. Smoked salmon cooked in the same way.

Boiled Salmon.

Salmon is boiled the same as halibut; served with egg sauce.

Fried Salmon.

The same as halibut.

Broiled Salmon.

The same as halibut.

Salmon Trout.

When large enough, split down the back, clean and broil. Season with butter and salt. When small, open far enough to take out the insides; wash clean, and wipe dry. Fry the same as cod fish.

Shad and Haddock.

Shad and haddock can be cooked the same as cod.

Fresh Mackerel Boiled.

If not cleaned, open them at the gills, take out the insides, wash clean, and pin in a fish-cloth. (Do not use the cloth that you use to boil mackerel in for any other fish.) Drop into boiling water, and boil fifteen minutes. Serve with drawn butter.

Broiled Mackerel.

Split down the back and clean. Be careful to scrape all the thin black skin from the inside. Wipe dry and lay on the gridiron; broil on one side a nice brown, then turn and brown the other side; it will not take so long to brown the side on which the skin is. (All fish should have the side on which the skin is, turned to the fire last, as the skin burns easily, and coals are not so hot after you have used them ten minutes.) Season with butter, pepper, and salt.

Fried Mackerel.

Fry brown six good-sized slices of pork. Prepare your mackerel as for broiling. Take out your pork, sprinkle a little salt over the mackerel, then fry a nice brown. Serve the fried pork with it.

Baked Mackerel.

Prepare as for boiling. Make a dressing as for baked cod. Stuff with this, dredge with salt and flour. Bake thirty minutes, basting often with water, butter, and flour. Make a gravy with the water in the pan in which the fish is baked. Always make the gravy quite salt. The best way to cook mackerel is to *broil* it.

To Broil and Fry Salt Mackerel.

Soak over night, and cook the same as fresh.

Salt Mackerel in Cream.

Freshen as for broiled mackerel, then lay into a baking pan, and to one mackerel add half a pint of new milk, put into the oven, and bake twenty-five minutes. About five minutes before it is dished, add a small piece of butter. This is a nice dish for breakfast and dinner.

To Boil Salt Mackerel.

Wash the mackerel, and soak over night in clear cold water. Put them on to boil in *cold* water, and boil gently thirty minutes. Serve with drawn butter.

Smelts.

The only true way to cook smelts is to fry them, although they are sometimes baked. Open them at the gills. Draw each smelt separately between your finger and thumb, beginning at the tail; this will press the insides out. (Some persons never take out the insides, but it should be done as much as in any other fish.) Wash them clean, and let them drain in a cullender; then salt and roll in a mixture half flour and half Indian meal. Have about two inches deep of boiling fat in the frying-pan (drippings if you have them; if not, lard); into this drop the smelts, and fry brown. Do not put so many in that they will be crowded; if you do, they will not be crisp and brown.

Brook Trout.

Brook trout are cooked the same as smelts: or you can

cook them as the angler does. They must be split nearly to the tail to clean. Wash and drain. For a dozen good-sized trout, fry six slices of salt pork; when brown, take out the pork, and put in the trout. Fry a nice brown on all sides. Serve the pork with them.

To Boil Lobster.

There are comparatively few who ever have anything to do with a lobster until after it has been boiled; but for the benefit of the few I insert this. Be sure that the lobster is living; if not, it is not fit for use. Have a kettle of *boiling* water; into this drop the lobster, and boil until the shell turns red. This takes about an hour. Take up, and when cold it is fit to eat.

Stewed Lobster.

Take out all the meat from the shell. Chop it, but not fine. Put into a basin with a little salt, pepper, butter, and half a cup of water to a small lobster. Stew about ten minutes.

Curried Lobster.

Prepare the lobster as for stew; when it comes to a boil, add a mixture of a heaping teaspoonful of flour, and half a teaspoonful of Indian curry mixed with cold water. Let this boil eight minutes, then serve.

Eels Fried.

Skin them;. then turn on boiling water, and let them

stand in it a few moments; then cut them into pieces about three inches long. Fry a nice brown, and serve.

Baked Eels.

Prepare as for frying; then put into a baking-pan, with a little water, flour, pepper, and salt. Bake twenty minutes. Make a gravy of the liquor in which they were baked, adding a little butter.

Remarks in regard to Fish.

Fish should never stand in water, as it spoils the flavor. Fish should never be fried in butter. It should always be used while fresh. Plain boiled or mashed potatoes should always be served with it. Squash and green peas go very well with fish also. Always save all that remains after a meal, and warm up, to help out another dish. The remains of boiled fresh fish can be warmed up in a little butter, pepper, salt, and water, as you would stew lobster. Cold fried and broiled fish can be placed in a tin pan, and set into the oven ten minutes, when it will be found to be hot enough. Fish balls can be steamed for ten or fifteen minutes, and then set into the oven to get crisp. If you have a large piece of boiled fish, which you wish to serve whole, place it on a plate, and set into the steamer, and steam twenty minutes. If you have drawn butter to warm up, do not set it on the fire, but put it into a bowl, and set the bowl into hot water. Cook butter as little as possible, as by cooking it becomes oily. When you do use it, always add it three or five minutes before taking the dish from the fire.

SOUPS.

Beef Soup.

Every family should have a soup once a week at least. Always save the bones of roast meats for a soup. Take the bones of a roast of beef, break them up so that they will go into a soup-pot. Lay them in the pot, dredge with salt, pepper, and flour. Cut into this one small onion; add three quarts of cold water. Set on the fire, and when it comes to a boil, skim it. Let it boil gently three hours, then add eight sliced potatoes, and boil twenty minutes. Have ready dumplings; put them in and cover tight, and boil ten minutes longer, then dish. First take out the dumplings and place in a small platter, then turn the soup into a tureen, being careful to take out the bones, and serve.

Mutton Broth.

Take a shoulder or neck of mutton, cut into small pieces, wash and put into the soup-pot. When it comes to a boil, skim it carefully; then boil gently two hours. To four pounds of meat add four quarts of water, and half a cup of rice. Do not put in the rice until the meat has boiled two hours, then add rice, and season with pepper, salt, and half an onion; boil two hours longer, and serve. I will give another method, which is better if the soup is the only dish for dinner.

Mutton Broth. No 2.

Prepare the meat as for No. 1, and to the same quantity of meat and water add half an onion, one small white turnip; boil two hours, then add one third of a cup of rice; boil one hour and a half longer, then add six sliced potatoes. Season to taste with pepper and salt. Boil twenty minutes, then add the dumplings; cover tight and boil ten minutes, then dish and serve as you would beef soup. When preparing the meat for all these kinds of soups, cut off all the fat, and fry out for dripping; thus your soup will not be greasy, and you will have the fat free from the taste of vegetables.

Dumplings for Soup.

Take one pint of flour (measured before it is sifted), turn into a seive, and measure into it one teaspoonful of cream of tartar, one half of saleratus, one half of salt, and one of sugar. Run this through the sieve, and wet with milk; have the dough stiff enough to roll. Cut into very small cakes, and cook ten minutes. Be sure that your soup boils fast enough to get up a good steam, and keep boiling while the dumplings are in the pot; if you do not, they will be heavy. Some persons like them for a dessert. When used for that purpose, they should be eaten with sirup.

Veal Soup.

Take four pounds of the neck of veal, cut up small and wash clean; put into the soup-pot and cover with six quarts of water; let this come to a boil, then skim off all the scum; boil two hours, add half a cup of rice, and boil one hour longer; then add one third of a cup of flour mixed with water, salt, and pepper. Boil gently one and a half hours, stirring often to prevent burning; then add a tablespoonful of butter, and dumplings made as directed for beef and mutton soup. Potatoes and onions can be used as for mutton broth No. 2, and some use a little pork to flavor it.

Pea Soup.

Pick the peas over, that there may be no blemished ones among them. Wash and soak over night. In the morning turn off the water and put them in the soup-pot. For one quart of peas allow eight quarts of cold water and one pound of lean salt pork, a small piece of celery, a little pepper, and half an onion; boil gently eight hours, being very careful that it does not burn. Have a large wooden spoon to stir it with. When done, it should be thin enough to pour. In boiling, it may become too thick; if so, add boiling water. When cooked, it is smooth and rather mealy. If not cooked enough, after standing a few minutes the thick part will settle, and the top look watery. Have ready six slices of bread toasted brown, and cut into pieces an inch square; throw about a dozen of these pieces into a tureen, and the remainder send to the table dry. Strain the soup through a sieve, and serve. If the pork does not salt it enough, use salt. This soup is even better warmed over than at first. Some persons use soup stock and butter, but it seems to me that it is rich enough made in this way, and much healthier.

The bones left from roast lamb, mutton, and veal can all be used to make soups the same as those of roast beef.

MEATS.

Boiled Corned Beef.

WASH a piece of beef weighing ten pounds; put it into two gallons of cold water; when it comes to a boil, skim carefully and boil very slowly six hours. Some boil all kinds of vegetables in the same pot; but there is this objection to this method; you lose the distinctive flavor of each vegetable, and the beef is flavored with the vegetables, which is very unpleasant when it is cold. The vegetables to serve with corned beef are potatoes, cabbage, beets, turnips, parsnips, carrots. When the beef is simply for one hot dinner, the part of the beef is not of so much consequence; but when it is to be pressed, there should be care taken in the selection of the piece to boil. The brisket, the flank, and the thin part of the ribs are the best parts to press. Boil as before directed, and take out the bones, lay the meat on a large platter, and place a tin sheet upon it; on the sheet place a weight, and set in a cool place. When ready to use it, trim the edges, and use the trimmings for meat hash. This makes a nice dinner with baked potatoes, squash, turnip, and macaroni.

Boiled Salt Tongue.

Soak the tongue over night; in the morning put on to boil in six quarts of cold water, and boil slowly six hours if the tongue is large; if not, five will answer. Take it from the boiling water and throw it into *cold* water, and peel the skin off. Set away to cool. For dinner, use the same vegetables as for cold corned beef. The roots will make a nice hash.

Boiled Fresh Tongue.

Wash and put into four quarts of boiling water, with a large handful of salt. Boil slowly six hours, if large. When done, throw into cold water and skin the same as the salt tongue. The water in which all meats are boiled should be saved until cold, and the fat should be taken off and clarified. The liquor should never stand in iron kettles, as it rusts them.

Boiled Flank of Beef.

This is a part of the beef that many persons think almost useless; but by being properly prepared it makes an elegant dish. Wash the flank, and make a dressing as for turkey, and spread over it, first having salted and peppered it well, then roll up and tie. Wind the twine round it several times, to keep it in place; then sew in a cloth kept for that purpose. Put a small plate in the pot, and put in the meat; then pour on about six quarts of boiling water, and boil gently six hours. When done, remove the cloth, but not the twine until stone cold; then cut into thin slices, and you will have alternate layers of meat and dressing. This is a very nice dish for breakfast or tea.

Boiled Ham.

Have a coarse hair brush for cleaning hams, as it is impossible to get them clean by simply washing them. If the ham will not fit in the pot, cut off the knuckles, which will cook in two hours. Cover with cold water, and boil. A ham weighing twelve pounds will require five hours. When cooked, take up and put into a baking pan, to skin. Have a basin of cold water, into which dip the hands; then take the skin between the fingers, and peel as you would an orange. Roll a cracker and sift it over the ham, then set in the oven thirty minutes. Save the liquor in which it has been boiled, and skim the fat for soap grease.

Boiled Leg of Mutton.

Take a leg weighing eight pounds, and put into six quarts of boiling water; throw into this half a cup of rice. In a few minutes a scum will rise, which must be skimmed off carefully. Boil one hour and a quarter; allow five minutes more for every pound over eight. This time will allow the blood to run, which should always be the case with mutton. Serve with caper sauce. The rice gives it a white look. Serve with this plain boiled potatoes, turnips, and onions. Save the liquor in which the meat was boiled, for soup.

Boiled Shoulder of Mutton.

Cooked and served the same as the leg.

Boiled Leg or Shoulder of Lamb.

For a leg or shoulder weighing six pounds, allow an hour and twenty minutes, and for every pound over that allow ten minutes. Serve with drawn butter or mint sauce. Serve with it green peas, potatoes, white turnips. If asparagus or spinage is in season, substitute for turnips Save the liquor for soup. Lamb, however, is always nicer roasted.

Boiled Fowl and Pork.

Singe, draw out the inwards, being careful to take out the lights and crop. Cut open the gizzard and clean. Wash the fowls and put them, with the hearts, livers, and gizzards, into boiling water, in which about one pound of pork has been boiling three hours. If they are young and tender, one hour and a quarter will cook one weighing three pounds. If old and tough, they sometimes take three hours Truss the same as turkey. Serve with drawn butter. Dish the pork with the fowls. A little rice boiled in the water give them a white appearance. Serve with them mashed turnip, mashed potatoes, boiled parsnips or green peas, corn or spinage when in season. Save the liquor for soup.

MEATS. 39

Boiled Veal.

Take out the bone from a shoulder of veal, and fill the cavity with a dressing made as for poultry; then fasten together with a skewer; wind twine around it, and tie tight. Put this into a kettle with about a pound of lean salt pork, and cover with boiling water. Boil slowly four hours, if it weighs ten pounds. Serve with celery sauce, or with a gravy made with one pint of the liquor in which it has been boiled, thickening with one heaping spoonful of flour, salt, pepper, and a little butter. Serve with boiled potatoes, macaroni and cheese, and horseradish. Save the liquor in which it has been boiled, to use next day in making a pie with what remains from the dinner.

Boiled Turkey.

Singe and wash the turkey, then rub into it a handful of salt; stuff it with a dressing made by directions given under "Dressing for Poultry." Sew up and put into boiling water, enough to cover it. For one weighing ten pounds allow two hours boiling, and fifteen minutes for every added pound. Serve with oyster or celery sauce, mashed potatoes, mashed turnips, boiled parsnips, plain boiled macaroni. Save the liquor for a soup. Sometimes a turkey will be very old and tough, in which case it will require a longer time to boil; but a little practice and observation will help every housekeeper to understand when to allow more or less time for boiling. *Truss the same as for roasting.*

Roast Beef.

Meats roasted in a tin kitchen require a longer time to cook than in an oven, but they are very much nicer cooked in the former. Wring a clean towel out of cold water, and wipe the meat with it (if possible, never wash beef, as by this means a great deal of juice is lost); then rub into it a handful of salt, and dredge with flour. If cooked in a tin oven, run the spit through it. See that the spit is as near through the middle as possible; if not, it will be difficult to turn it. Dredge flour into the kitchen, and when brown put in a pint of hot water. Cook a piece of beef weighing eight pounds an hour and twenty minutes if you wish it rare; if not, cook twenty minutes longer. Baste often with pepper, salt, flour, and the water in the bottom of the kitchen, and turn often. Ten minutes before dishing the dinner, turn the gravy into a basin, and skim of *all the fat;* let it come to a boil, and thicken with one large table-spoonful of flour mixed with cold water; season with salt and pepper. Serve with mashed potatoes, squash, boiled rice, and pickled beets. When baked in the oven, one hour will be sufficient for a piece weighing eight pounds. Place a grate in the baking-pan, and upon the grate lay the meat. Into the pan pour a pint of warm water; watch carefully that the water does not boil away and the gravy become burned. Add but little water at a time, for if there is too much the meat will be steamed instead of roasted, and also the gravy will not become brown. Baste as when roasted in a tin oven. Make the gravy as before directed.

Roast Mutton.

Take out the first joint from a leg of mutton; ask the butcher to do it when you order it. Wash, and rub into it a handful of salt. Cut in around the bone, so as to make the cavities as large as possible, and fill with a dressing made in the following manner: Soak in *cold* water about two quarts of pieces of stale bread. When soft, drain in a cullender; then mix with this half an onion, which has been chopped *very fine*, one teaspoonful of pepper, one tablespoonful of salt, one egg, butter the size of an egg, and one tablespoonful of summer savory. Fasten together with a skewer, then dredge with salt and flour, and roast the same as beef. For a piece weighing ten pounds allow one hour and a half, and ten minutes for every pound over or under that. Skim *all* the fat from the gravy; for half a pint allow one tablespoonful of flour to thicken with; season with pepper and salt. Put one tablespoonful of currant jelly into the gravy tureen, and strain the gravy upon it. Serve with mashed potatoes, boiled onions, boiled rice or macaroni, mashed turnip, currant jelly.

When the tin kitchen is used it will require half an hour longer to roast. The shoulder and saddle are cooked in the same way. Always make a dressing for mutton; it spends much better, and the trouble is not much. Omit the egg if you please. When you do not stuff it, cook it in twenty minutes less time.

Roast Lamb.

Take a leg of lamb weighing six pounds, wash and dredge with salt and flour. Cook one hour if in an oven, one and a quarter if in a tin kitchen. Baste often. Make the gravy the same as for mutton, omitting the jelly. Serve with mashed potatoes, green peas, fried parsnips, or green corn, string beans, summer squash, mint sauce. Never omit the gravy because you have mint sauce. All other parts of the lamb can be roasted in the same way.

Roast Veal.

The loin, breast, and fillet are the best parts for roasting; the neck also is good to roast. Wash the veal, and rub into it a good handful of salt. Make a dressing in the following manner, and stuff it: Soak about two quarts of stale bread in cold water, chop fine half a pound of clear fat pork. Mix this with the bread and one teaspoonful of pepper, one of salt, one tablespoonful of sweet marjorum, one of sage, one egg or two rolled crackers. Take out all the bones possible, and cut slits to make cavities for the dressing; then stuff and skewer securely; dredge with salt, pepper and flour. Have thin slices of salt pork, which lay on the top of the veal. Cook a piece weighing twelve pounds five hours, and baste *very often*. I should always roast veal in the oven. Make the gravy as for roast beef, but do not strain. If possible, always cook a large piece of veal, because so many nice dishes can be made from cold roast veal. Serve mashed potatoes, spinage, asparagus, fried parsnips, horseradish.

Roast Pork.

Wash and dredge a sparerib with salt, pepper, sage, and flour; and roast the same as beef. Cook a sparerib weighing ten pounds three hours, if cooked in a tin kitchen; if in the oven two hours and a half. Have the oven moderately hot. The chine to be cooked in the same way, allowing one hour longer for a piece weighing the same as a sparerib. Make the gravy as directed for roast beef. Serve potatoes, squash, fried or boiled onions, boiled rice, mashed turnips, applesauce.

Broiled Beefsteak.

Cut the steak about three quarters of an inch thick. Have a clear fire and lay the steak on the gridiron, and dredge lightly with flour. If you desire the steak rare, cook ten minutes; if well done, fifteen. Dish and season with butter, pepper and salt. Serve *immediately*. Never set steak into the oven to keep warm or to melt the butter. The dish must be hot, the butter stand in a warm room long enough to soften but do not *melt*. If for dinner, serve potatoes, either baked or boiled and any other vegetables which you choose. Many persons pound tough steak before cooking, but I would not recommend it, as by this means it looses much of its juiciness.

There are some families in the country who have no means of broiling. The next best thing such persons can do is to heat the frying-pan very hot, and grease with just enough butter to prevent the steak from sticking; then lay the steak in, and cook, and serve as before directed.

Fried Beefsteak.

For two pounds of steak fry brown four slices of salt pork, then take up the pork and fry the steak in the fat; salt and pepper it. When you dish add a little butter. To the fat remaining in the frying-pan, after the steak has been cooked, add one tablespoonful of *dry* flour (be sure to have the fat boiling), and stir until it is brown and there are no lumps, then pour in about half a cup of boiling water. Season well with pepper and salt. Serve in a gravy tureen. This is a more economical, but not so healthy a method as broiling.

Beefsteak Smothered in Onions.

Fry brown four slices of salt pork; when brown take out the pork, and put in six onions sliced thin Fry about ten minutes, stirring all the while; then take out all except a thin layer, and upon this lay a slice of steak, then a layer of onions, then steak, and cover thick with onions. Dredge each layer with pepper, salt and flour. Pour over this one cupful of boiling water, and cover tight. Simmer half an hour. When you dish, place the steak in the centre of the dish,

MEATS. 45

and heap the onions around it. Serve the same vegetables as for broiled steak.

Italianed Beef.

Broil the steak as before directed; place in the dish and cover with onions prepared in the following manner: Slice very thin four good-sized onions, and fry in pork fat thirty minutes, then add half a cup of boiling water, cover tight, and simmer thirty minutes longer. While frying, season with pepper, salt and a little butter. Vegetables the same as for broiled steak.

Stewed Beef.

Take a piece of beef that is rather tough, or pieces of tough beefsteak; rub into it a handful of salt, some pepper and flour; lay in a kettle that you can cover tight, and that has a flat bottom. Cut up an onion, a potato, a *small* turnip, a carrot and a parsnip; lay these on the top of the meat and then sprinkle in half a teaspoonful of cinnamon, half of mace, one fourth of clove, and add cold water enough to cover it. Let it come to a boil, skim off all the scum, then cover tight, and simmer five hours. After it has been boiling four hours, mix half a cup of flour with cold water and add to it. You can then taste it, and add more seasoning if necessary. The spice may be omitted if you choose. Serve the meat in a little of the gravy, and send the remainder of the gravy to the table in the gravy-tureen. Serve plain boiled potatoes, boiled rice, and pickled beets.

Fricassee of Beef.

Put one pint of water into a frying-pan, and when it comes to a boil, thicken with one heaping spoonful of flour; season with salt, pepper and a little butter. Cut cold roast beef into slices, and put into this gravy, and let them boil five minutes. If there be any cold beef gravy, add it to the other, in which case you will not need quite so much butter. Serve boiled potatoes, tomatoes, boiled rice or macaroni and squash.

Mutton Chops.

Cut the chops from the loin or the neck; broil as you do beefsteak, and serve in *hot* dishes. Serve mashed potatoes, stewed tomatoes, boiled onions and boiled rice.

Mutton Pie with Tomatoes.

Pare and slice six tomatoes; put a layer into a deep pudding dish, then put in a layer of slices of cold mutton, and dredge in flour, salt and pepper. Have the last layer tomatoes, over which sprinkle two rolled crackers. Bake one hour. Serve boiled potatoes, boiled rice, green corn, shelled beans.

Mutton Pie, Plain.

Take the cold mutton that has remained from a former dinner, cut into thin slices, put into a pudding dish, and season with pepper and salt. Mix two tablespoonfuls of flour with cold water, then pour onto this one pint of *boiling* water, and season with pepper and salt, then pour this over the meat. Make a paste by rule for plain piecrust, and cover it. Bake one hour. Vegetables the same as for pie, with tomatoes, with the addition of stewed tomatoes.

Mutton Fricassee.

Mutton fricassee is made the same as beef. Heap the meat in the centre of the dish, and garnish the sides with boiled rice. Send to the table very hot. Serve mashed potatoes, mashed turnips, baked tomatoes and shelled beans.

Haricot of Mutton.

Take cold mutton (either boiled or roasted), cut into slices, and lay in a deep sauce-pan, and then put in one fourth of an onion, the same of turnip, and two potatoes, and one carrot, all cut into small pieces. Dredge with flour, salt and pepper. Cover with cold water, and boil slowly one hour; then add two spoonfuls of flour mixed with cold water, and boil one hour longer. Have a dish ready with an edging of mashed potatoes (brown them or not, as you please), and into the centre of the dish turn the haricot. Serve mashed potatoes, boiled rice, mashed turnips and carrots.

Minced Mutton.

Take all the fat from cold mutton, and then put it into the chopping-tray; dredge well with salt, pepper, and flour, and then chop (do not chop it very fine); then put into a sauce-pan, and to two pounds of meat allow one cup of boiling water and a spoonful of butter. Let it boil gently fifteen minutes, and dish on toast. This is a nice dish for breakfast or dinner.

Lamb Chops.

Broil fifteen minutes over clear coals. Season with butter, pepper, and salt.

Broiled Veal.

Cut veal into thin slices, and broil twenty minutes. Season with butter, pepper, and salt. This is the most unsavory method of cooking veal, and I would not recommend it.

Fricassee of Veal.

Fry eight slices of salt pork brown. Take out the pork and put in *thin* slices of veal which have been cut from the leg. Sprinkle with salt and pepper, and fry *brown*. When all the veal is fried, mix with the boiling fat two tablespoonfuls of *dry* flour; stir until there are no lumps, and the flour is brown; then add two cups of boiling water, and season with salt and pepper. Lay the veal in this gravy, and simmer fifteen minutes. Dish and pour the gravy over the meat. If for dinner, garnish with boiled rice, and serve plain boiled potatoes, spinage, and horseradish.

Veal Cutlets.

Fry brown eight slices of salt pork. Take them up, and add to the fat two large spoonfuls of lard or drippings. Have ready thin slices of veal (they are best cut from the leg), dip them in an egg which has been well beaten, then into cracker crumbs, and fry a nice brown. Season them, before dipping in the egg and cracker, with pepper and salt. Serve with the salt pork. If for dinner, serve mashed potatoes, boiled or stewed parnips, and horscradish.

Veal on Toast.

Chop the veal as for mutton Mince and season in the same manner. Use a little more water, and boil fifteen minutes; dish on toast, and garnish with thin slices of lemon. This is a nice dish for either dinner or breakfast.

Veal Croquettes.

Chop cold veal fine (boiled is the nicest), season with pepper and salt, and to a quart of veal, after it is chopped, add half a cup of warm water (when chopping the veal, dredge in flour as for veal on toast), form this into egg shapes about the size of an egg, and dip into a well-beaten egg, then roll in cracker crumbs, and fry, as you would doughnuts, in hot lard.

Pork Steak.

Cut pork steak quite thin, and sprinkle with salt, pepper, and a *little* powdered sage. Put a spoonful of drippings or lard in the pan, and lay the pork in it; fry slowly fifteen minutes. Always be sure that the meat is cooked until white at the centre; if it has a pink appearance, it is not done. If for dinner, serve boiled potatoes, squash, boiled onions, and apple-sauce.

Fried Salt Pork.

Cut salt pork into slices a quarter of an inch thick, cut off the rind, and then pour over them boiling water, in which let them stand ten minutes; then turn off the water, and fry until they are brown on both sides.

Broiled Salt Pork.

Prepare as for fried, and broil ten minutes over clear coals.

Salt Pork Fried in Batter.

Fry the pork as before directed; dip in batter, and fry in the pork fat, to which should be added two spoonfuls of drippings or lard. Make the batter in the following manner: Mix gradually with one cup of flour, one cup of milk, and then add one well-beaten egg and a little salt. This makes a pleasant change in the

MEATS. 51

country, where it is so difficult to get fresh meat. Serve potatoes and any other vegetable that you please.

Fried Sausages.

Cut the sausages apart and wash them; then lay them in the pan and pour boiling water over them; let them boil two minutes, then turn off the water and prick the sausages with a fork, or they will burst open when they begin to fry. Put a little drippings in the pan with them, and fry twenty minutes. Turn them often that they may be brown on all sides. Cut stale bread into fanciful shapes, fry in the sausage fat, and garnish the dish with it. Brown bread is delicious fried in this way. Serve plain boiled potatoes, squash, mashed turnips, and applesauce.

Broiled Sausages.

Scald as for fried, and broil as you would any other kind of meat. Sausages that are kept a long time become dry and hard; they are very much improved by covering them with boiling water in which half a teaspoonful of saleratus has been dissolved, and boiling twenty minutes before frying them.

Pigs' Feet Soused.

Scrape and wash the pigs' feet. Clean them, cover them with salt and water, and let them stand two days; then turn this water off, and cover again with fresh salt and water; let them stand two days longer, then boil about two hours. When cold, split them, and pour over them boiling vinegar, in which there have been thrown a few whole cloves, a piece of stick cinnamon, and a handful of salt. They will be ready for use in twenty-four hours.

Fried Pigs' Feet.

Put into the frying-pan four spoonfuls of drippings or lard, and when this boils, lay in the feet, first having dredged them with flour, and fry brown. Serve on hot dishes. They can be fried before or after being soused. Never season them with butter.

Pigs' Feet Fried in Batter.

Take the feet from the vinegar and drain them, then dip them in a batter made as for pork, and fry in either drippings or lard.

Pigs' Head Cheese.

Boil a pigs' head until the bones will drop out. When cold, chop fine and season highly with pepper, salt, and sage; then put it into a kettle, and to every quart of meat add one half a pint of the liquor in which it was boiled. Simmer this slowly for half an hour, and turn it into deep earthen dishes, and on top place a plate with a weight upon it. Set in a cool place, and when cold cut in slices. If there is any danger of its not keeping, scald it over. Many persons put spice in it, but it is more natural without.

Fried Ham.

Cut the ham in very *thin* slices, and cut off the rind. Have half a spoonful of boiling drippings in the frying-pan, lay the ham in this, and fry quickly eight minutes; it will then be brown and crisp. Where the ham is for dinner, have the slices larger and thicker, and if you do not have eggs with it, fry bread, as directed for sausages.

Broiled Ham.

Cut the ham in thin slices; cut off the rind, and broil over clear coals ten minutes. Butter or not, as you please. When the ham is very salt or hard, slice, and let stand in boiling water ten minutes before frying or broiling.

Ham and Eggs.

Fry the ham as before directed, and when the ham is all fried, turn the fat into a basin, and scrape the salt from the frying-pan; turn back the fat, and add to it half a cup of lard. When this comes to a boil, break in your eggs, leaving room to turn them, if you prefer them turned; they look much nicer, however, when they are not turned. If they are not turned, dip up the boiling fat while they are cooking and pour over them; they will cook rare in three minutes, well done in four. Lay them on the slices of ham, and serve.

Fried Liver.

Cut either beef or pork liver into slices about half an inch thick, and pour boiling water over them, in which let them stand twenty minutes; then drain, and dredge with flour, salt, and pepper. Fry six slices of pork brown; take them up, and in the fat fry the liver fifteen minutes. Serve the pork with it.

Broiled Liver.

Prepare as for frying, and broil fifteen minutes over clear coals. Season with butter, salt, and pepper. When for dinner, serve boiled or baked potatoes, squash, and macaroni.

Boiled Tripe.

Wash a tripe clean (it must be washed in several waters), and boil ten hours. Turn it often, as it is apt to stick to the bottom. After it has boiled seven hours, throw a cupful of salt into the boiler with it. When eaten plain boiled, cut up in squares, and serve with seasoning of salt, pepper, and butter.

Broiled Tripe.

Cut the tripe after it has become cold, into handsome squares; grease the gridiron, and broil ten minutes. Season with salt, pepper, and butter. Serve on very hot dishes. If you buy tripe, get the honeycomb, as that is the nicest part of it.

Fried Tripe.

Cut into handsome squares, and dredge with salt, pepper, and flour, and fry a light brown, in either drippings or lard.

Soused Tripe.

Cut the tripe into squares, and lay them in an earthen pot, and pour over them boiling vinegar enough to cover, in which a blade of mace, a dozen whole cloves, and a stick of cinnamon have been boiled. It will be ready for use in twelve hours, and will keep several weeks. Soused tripe may be either broiled, or fried plain, or in batter.

Tripe Fried in Batter.

Drain the tripe, and make a batter as for pigs' feet; dip the tripe in this, and fry in hot drippings or lard. Tripe is nice cooked in this manner, either before or after it has been soused.

Calf's Head and Pluck.

Take out the brains, and lay them in a dish of cold water. Scrape the head and wash, then lay in a tub of cold water two hours; then put into a pot with two gallons of cold water. Tie the brains in a cloth, and boil with the head. When it comes to a boil, skim carefully. When it has boiled two hours, put in the heart, liver, and feet, and boil two hours longer. When you dish, take the bones from the head, and place it in the centre of the dish. Cut some slices from the heart and liver, and place around the head. Split the feet, and lay on the edge of the dish. Serve with brain sauce. To make the brain sauce, braid together the brains, half a teacup of flour, one teaspoonful of pepper, two of salt, one of parsley, one of summer savory. Pour on this one pint and a half of boiling water, and let it boil twenty minutes, then add one cup of butter and the juice of two lemons, and boil five minutes longer. You may omit the herbs if you choose. A piece of salt pork boiled with the head and pluck is an improvement, but it is not necessary. The tongue is nice cut in thin slices and served cold. The heart, liver, and head make a nice hash. Save the liquor to make soup, which may be made plain or mock turtle.

Hash Made from Calf's Head and Pluck.

Chop together parts of the head, liver, and heart, in the proportion of one third each. Season with pepper, salt, a little fresh lemon or a little vinegar. Warm in just enough of the liquor in which it was boiled, to moisten it. Just before dishing stir in a little butter. Serve on toast.

Meat Hash.

Chop fine any kind of cold meat (before chopping

dredge with salt and pepper This is always the best manner of seasoning hash, as by this means all parts will be seasoned alike). If you have cold potatoes, *chop* fine and mix with the meat, if they are *hot*, mash. Allow one third meat to two thirds potato. Put this mixture in the frying-pan with a little water to moisten it, and stir in a spoonful of butter, or, if you have nice beef drippings, use that instead of butter. Heat slowly, stirring often, and when warmed through, cover and let it stand on a moderately hot part of the stove or range twenty minutes. When ready to dish, fold as you would an omelet, and dish. Save all the trimmings and pieces that are left of all kinds of meat, and have a hash once or twice a week. It does not hurt a hash to have different kinds of meat in it. Avoid having a hash (or indeed any other part of your cooking) greasy. It is a great mistake to think that seasoning anything highly with butter improves it; on the contrary, it often ruins it by disguising the natural flavor, and giving you an unhealthy dish. I have nothing to say against a moderate use of butter in cooking, but I do strongly protest against the immoderate use of it in soups, gravies, hashes, stews, and on meats and fish of all kinds. I do not know of one kind of soup that is improved by the addition of butter.

Observe, when you let steak stand in the oven or on the hearth a few minutes after buttering, you will find that the butter has become oily, and you have neither the flavor of the meat or butter, but an unpleasant oily flavor. I have given only the simplest modes of cooking meats in this department, and many may think, perhaps, that I have been too minute; but I have not forgotten the time when these little hints, as how to put things together, as well as the quantities and kinds to take, would have been of untold value to me; and I know that every day there are young housekeepers, and young girls who have to work in young housekeepers' kitchens, who need just these little hints to make the simplest dishes what they should be. For soups, poultry, and richer methods of cooking meats, look in the department for rich **cooking.**

VEGETABLES.

Boiled Potatoes.

IF the potatoes are new, wash clean and put into boiling water; boil thirty minutes, and serve immediately. As they grow older, scrape the skin off before boiling. For old potatoes, have a sharp knife with a thin blade, and pare the potatoes, having the skin as thin as possible. They are very much better if they stand in cold water a few hours before boiling; then put them in boiling water and boil thirty minutes. When they have boiled fifteen minutes, throw in a handful of salt. When done, turn off the water and let them stand on the back part of the range three minutes, then shake them up once and turn into the dish, and send to the table.

Mashed Potatoes.

Prepare and boil as for plain, and then mash. To two dozen potatoes add one cup of boiling milk and one spoonful of butter. If they are not salt enough, add a little more. They should be dished as soon as mashed. Heap them in the dish in an oval form, smooth and indent with the knife.

Browned Potatoes.

Prepare and mash as for plain mashed potatoes; then heap them in an oval form on a buttered tin sheet. Smooth with a knife, and then dip the knife in milk and smooth over again, wetting every part with the milk, and place in the oven to brown; they will brown in twenty minutes in a hot oven. I would not recommend browning potatoes, as the moisture, being baked in, spoils the flavor and renders them clammy. They look handsome made into pear shapes and browned.

Baked Potatoes.

Be very particular to wash every part of the potato clean, as many persons eat the skin. Put them in a pan (have an old one for this purpose), and bake in a moderate oven fifty minutes. There is such a difference in ovens that each one must learn for herself what the time will be for each; for some will bake in less time, and some will take much longer than the time designated.

Fried Potatoes.

Pare and slice *thin* raw potatoes, and let them stand in cold water several hours; if in summer, put a piece of ice in the water. Cut the slices *lengthwise* of the potato. Have ready a basin with *boiling* drippings or lard, drain the potatoes a minute in the cullender, and drop them into the boiling fat, and fry a light brown; take them out with a skimmer, and lay them in a dry cullender, which should be placed in a tin pan and set in an open oven. There should be as much fat as for frying doughnuts, and there should not be any more potatoes put in at a time than will fry brown and not stick together. Have the basin in which you fry quite deep, as there is danger of the fat boiling over when the potatoes are put in. When you take the potatoes up, dredge a little salt over them. When potatoes are cooked in this manner, they will be light and crisp. If they do not get cooked enough at first, they are very much improved by dropping them into the fat for one minute, after they have been standing in the oven a while.

Fried Boiled Potatoes.

Cut the potatoes into slices, and fry in either pork fat or nice drippings. Have just fat enough in the pan to prevent their sticking, and sprinkle with salt while cooking. When these are brown, take them up and put in a little more fat, and fry as before.

Potatoes warmed with Pork.

Cut about eight slices of pork into pieces about half an inch square, and fry a nice brown. Have ready one dozen cold potatoes cut into slices, and turn them into the pan with the fried pork, and dredge in a little salt and pepper, then stir and cut them into small pieces with the knife. When a light brown, serve.

Potatoes warmed in Gravy.

Slice cold potatoes as for frying, and turn them into the frying-pan, and to a dozen potatoes add a pint of cold gravy. Season with pepper and salt, and stir, and cut with a knife, until they are hot and in *small* pieces.

Fricassee of Potatoes.

Cut cold boiled potatoes into small squares, and put them in a basin with milk, pepper, and salt, allowing half a pint of milk to a dozen potatoes. Set the basin into another of hot water, and when it comes to a boil, add a table spoonful of butter, and set on the stove, and let it boil up once, then serve.

Boiled Sweet Potatoes.

Wash and boil, with the skins on, forty-five minutes. They are much better baked than boiled, and I would cook them so generally.

Baked Sweet Potatoes.

Wash and wipe dry, and bake one hour. Do not cook squash when you have sweet potatoes.

Boiled Onions.

When new and tender, they will boil in one hour; but after the month of October, they will require two hours. Put them into water before peeling them, and they will not affect the eyes. Peel of all the dark skin, and put them in hot water, and boil as directed. If you have milk plenty, half an hour before they are done, turn a quart into the water in which they are boiling. This makes them white, and is said to prevent, in a measure, the disagreeable odor which always follows their being eaten. Boil them in a porcelain kettle. Dish them whole, and season with a little pepper, salt, and butter.

Fried Onions.

Peel and slice thin ten good-sized onions, and put them in a frying-pan with two spoonfuls of drippings. Fry thirty minutes, turning often.

Boiled Squash.

Cut the squash in strips, and cut out the soft, stringy part; pare, wash, and cover with boiling water; boil twenty-five minutes, then turn into a cullender for a few minutes, and when all the water is drained off, put it back in the basin with a little salt, pepper, and butter, and mash. Dish the same as mashed potatoes.

Baked Squash.

Cut the squash in two, take out of all the soft, stringy part; if you need the whole squash for dinner, lay the halves together, and put in a baking-pan (the old one you use for baking potates in), and bake forty-five minutes. When done, scrape the squash from the shell, and season, and serve as boiled squash. When you cook but half a squash, lay it with the inside downward. This is a nice way to cook watery squash. Squash is also good steamed. It will take forty-five minutes to steam.

Beets.

Wash clean, but do not scrape; if you do they will look white when cooked. When young they will cook in two hours; but old ones will require four or five hours. When done, plunge them into cold water, and the skin will peel off easily. Cut in thin slices, and lay in a flat dish.

Pickled Beets.

Cut the beets that are left from dinner into thin slices, and lay them in an earthen vessel, and cover with cold vinegar and a few whole cloves. Keep in a cold place.

Shelled Beans.

Wash in several waters, and put them in a basin with boiling water. Boil one hour. Do not drain them very dry. Season with butter and salt.

Baked Beans.

Examine and wash one quart of dry beans (the pea bean is the best), and put them in a pan with six quarts of cold water; let them soak in this over night. In the morning wash them in another water, and place them on the fire with six quarts of cold water and a pound of mixed salt pork. If they are the present year's beans, they will cook enough in half an hour; if older, one hour. Drain them and put half in the bean-pot; then gash the pork, and put in the remainder of the beans, one tablespoonful of molasses, and one of salt, and cover with boiling water. Bake ten hours. Watch them carefully, and do not let them cook dry.

String Beans.

String and cut into pieces about an inch long; then wash and put into boiling water, and boil one hour. Season with salt and butter.

Stewed Beans.

Wash and soak over night one quart of beans. (Scarlet runners are the best.) In the morning set them on the fire with six quarts of cold water and one and a half pounds of mixed salt pork. They will cook in four hours, but are better cooked five. Stir them often to prevent burning. Season with pepper before dishing, and if the pork does not season it enough, add a little salt.

Green Peas.

Put them into boiling water, and when very young they will cook in twenty minutes; but generally they require thirty. Season with salt and butter.

Green Corn.

Boil twenty-five minutes, if very young and tender. As it grows older it requires a longer time. Send to the table in a napkin.

Boiled Turnips.

Peel and cut into slices. If they are to be served in slices, boil with a small piece of pork. Boil the pork three hours, and put in the turnips; if they are the white turnip, they will cook in forty-five minutes; but if the yellow, they will require two hours. Serve in slices without any seasoning except what they get by being boiled with the pork. For mashed, cook in the same way, omitting the pork, and season with salt, pepper, and butter. When the white turnip is very watery, it is improved by mashing a few mealy potatoes with it. Dish as directed for mashed potato.

Boiled Parsnips.

Scrape very clean, and cut lengthwise into slices. Put them into a stew-pan, and cover with water, and boil one hour. Serve with a *little* drawn butter.

Fried Parsnips.

Prepare as before directed, and boil half an hour. Let them grow cold, and fry a light brown in pork fat (Never use butter to fry.) They are very nice cooked whole with a piece of pork, as you cook turnips. The time to eat parsnips is in April and May, and they should be dug fresh when used. Dig a large box full in the fall, and cover them with earth. Use these for soups; they are one of the nicest vegetables that there are for flavoring soups.

Boiled Carrots.

Prepare, boil, and serve the same as parsnips.

Boiled Rice.

Wash and pick all the specks from a cup of rice. Let it stand in cold water two hours, and then put it in a deep kettle, with two quarts of water, and boil *fast* thirty minutes. When it has boiled twenty minutes, throw in a great spoonful of salt. When done, turn into a cullender, and set in the oven a few minutes. When ready to dish, shake lightly and *turn* into the vegetable dish. Never use a spoon. If these directions are followed, you will have a handsome and healthy vegetable, and every kernel will be separate. The water in which the rice has been boiled makes a nice starch for colored clothes.

The southern rice cooks much quicker and is nicer than the Indian rice. If possible, always purchase the former.

Another Mode.

Wash one cupful of rice and put into a tin basin or pail, with three cupfuls of cold water, and a teaspoonful of salt, cover and set in another basin, with hot water.

place on the fire, and boil thirty minutes. Rice is very healthy, and should be a common dish on the table.

Stewed Tomatoes.

Pour boiling water over half a peck of ripe tomatoes. Let them stand in it five minutes, and then peel off the skins; cut them into slices, and put in a stew-pan with a little salt, pepper, and a spoonful of sugar. Simmer two hours, stirring often to prevent burning. Two minutes before dishing stir in one tablespoonful of butter. Canned tomatoes are cooked in the same manner, but do not require more than half an hour to stew.

Sliced Tomatoes.

Pour boiling water over them, and then peel and slice thin; lay them on small platters, and serve. Let each person season to his own taste.

Baked Tomatoes.

Scald and peel as directed; have ready an earthen dish, into which lay a layer of tomatoes (whole), then sprinkle with salt, pepper, and cracker crumbs; then another layer of tomatoes, and sprinkle again with salt and pepper. Cut a spoonful of butter into small pieces and lay on the tomatoes, and then cover with cracker crumbs. Bake thirty minutes.

VEGETABLES.

Asparagus.

Cut off the white part, wash and tie in small bunches, and put into a sauce-pan with boiling water enough to cover it, and a handful of salt. When young it will boil in twenty minutes; if not tender, boil thirty. Dish on toast, and season with a little butter.

Spinage.

Pick carefully and see that there are no weeds or grass in it; then wash in several waters. Put on to boil in boiling water, and boil an hour and a half. When about half done, throw into the water a spoonful of salt. When done, drain and put in a dish with a little butter, and cut it several times with a knife. Dish and garnish with slices of hard-boiled egg. You can boil it with a piece of salt pork, and then you will not require the butter and eggs.

Cabbage.

Cut the stalk and all the loose leaves from the cabbage; then cut the cabbage into four parts, and wash clean Examine it carefully, as there are worms in it sometimes. Put it in a deep pan, and pour *boiling* water over it, and let it stand in the shed (that it may not scent the house) half an hour. Boil with a small piece of salt pork two hours, or you can boil it with corned beef, as many persons do; but it has not the white appearance that it has when boiled with pork. When cold, it is nice warmed with a little of the drippings of corned beef.

Cauliflower.

Cut off the loose leaves and the stock; wash clean, and let it stand in cold water one hour; then put on to boil in boiling water, and if very large, boil one hour and a half; but if small, one hour will answer. When nearly done, stir in a spoonful of salt and half a pint of milk. Serve whole in a deep dish, and spread over it a little butter. The milk can be omitted, as its only use is to whiten the cauliflower.

Dandelions.

Pick over carefully, and wash in several waters; cut off all the roots, then put into boiling water, and boil one hour; then drain off this water, and again put them into boiling water, and boil two hours longer. Put a spoonful of salt into the second water. When done, turn into a cullender and drain; then season with butter and more salt if necessary, and cut them with a knife. Serve in a deep vegetable dish. They may be boiled with a piece of salt pork, but in that case omit the butter.

Beet Greens.

Scrape the roots and wash in several waters; then let them stand in cold water a few hours. Boil a small piece of salt pork three hours, then put the beet greens into the kettle with it, and boil one hour longer.

Macaroni Boiled.

Break up and wash a pint bowl full of macaroni, and put in a shallow basin, and cover with cold water. Set this basin into another of warm water, and place on the fire; after fifteen minutes, add a pint of milk and a teaspoonful of salt; let it cook ten minutes longer, then add a spoonful of butter, and cook five minutes more, and dish. Be careful not to break the macaroni in dishing. The boiled macaroni which remains from one dinner can be used for the next, by preparing it in the following manner: Butter a shallow dish, and turn the macaroni into it; then grate over it old cheese, and brown.

BREAD.

ALWAYS purchase the *best* flour; it is much cheaper than the low priced. Keep a large tin pan or wooden bowl full of sifted flour, and always keep the flour covered. Have two quarts, one for dry, and the other for liquid measuring. The old beer measure is the kind to get. If you buy milk, it will not do to consider the milkman's quart for any rule in this book. You must always measure with the beer measure. *Good bread* is the most *important* branch of cooking. Therefore I hope every housekeeper, who cannot already make good bread, will give particular attention to this branch before attending to cake or pastry of any kind. It seems as if enough had been written and said, in regard to this subject, to awaken every young woman to the importance of it; but it is not so. If a young lady learns to do any kind of cooking, it is cake and pastry, and if she learns to make bread, it is the *last* thing, instead of the first, to be learned. Now I certainly think that no girl should pass her eighteenth year without a practical knowledge of bread-making, cooking vegetables and plain meats. I have no objections to all the nice fancy cooking, which any one may learn afterwards; but have bread, vegetables, and meats *first*. When reading a rule for doing anything, it *seems*

as if the process were *longer* and *harder* than when the
'rule is very short. But I hope none will feel so because
I have gone into all the details, for I feel that it is because of the neglect of *the small* things that so many
fail in cooking, as in everything else.

Hop Yeast.

Pare and boil one dozen mealy potatoes (they will
boil in thirty minutes); as soon as you put the potatoes
on to boil, put a handful of hops into another kettle with
three quarts of *cold* water, cover and boil (watch it that
it may not boil over). When the potatoes are boiled,
drain and mash fine; then strain the hops through a
fine sieve on the potatoes (be sure that the hops are
boiling when they are strained on the potatoes), and stir
well; then add one half a cup of sugar, one fourth of
salt, and one pint of flour; mix this well and strain
through a cullender; let it stand until it is milk-warm,
then stir in one cup of good yeast, and set it to rise
where it will be warm. It will rise in five hours if the
yeast is good. You can tell when it is risen by the
white foam, which will rise to the top. When risen, put
it in a stone jug, and stop tight. It is a good plan to
tie the cork down, as it sometimes flies out. Set in the
ice chest or on the cellar bottom. Make one third this
quantity in summer if your family be small.

Hop Yeast, No. 2.

In the spring and the first of the summer, when
potatoes are poor, it is better to make yeast without

them. Boil one fourth of a cup of hops in one quart of water, and strain it upon a half a pint of flour; stir this well, and add two spoonfuls of sugar and one of salt, then strain through a cullender, and let it become milk-warm, when add one cup of good yeast. You need just as much yeast for one third the quantity made without potatoes, as you would for the whole made with potatoes. Rise and bottle the same as the preceding.

Potato Yeast.

Pare and boil six good-sized potatoes; when done, mash, and pour on them three pints of boiling water; run this through the cullender, and then stir in one spoonful of sugar and one of salt. When milk-warm, stir in half a cup of yeast. In summer time this will rise in three or four hours. It will not keep as long as hop yeast.

Yeast Bread.

Take four good-sized potatoes, peel, boil, and mash, and pour on to them one quart of *boiling* water; strain the whole through a sieve; let this get blood-warm, and then stir into it one cup of yeast, one spoonful of white sugar, one spoonful of salt, and three quarts and a pint of flour. Beat well with a spoon and set in a warm place to rise. (In the summer it will rise in four hours, in winter it will take five.) When well risen, take a pint of flour and put part of it on the kneading-board; then turn the dough upon the board, and put one spoonful of lard on it; then knead twenty minutes, using the pint of flour; now put the dough in the pan again, and let it rise one hour, and then form into loaves. (Do not have over a pint bowl full of dough in a loaf.) Let the loaves rise forty minutes, and bake forty-five minutes. Bread made in this way cannot be excelled; the only objection to it is that you have to bake in the afternoon; but when good bread is wanted, a little extra work should not prevent it being made.

Yeast Bread, No. 2.

Make a hole in the middle of four quarts of flour, into which turn one spoonful of sugar, one of salt, and one cup of yeast; then mix with one pint of cold milk, which has been warmed by the addition of one pint of boiling water, and add one spoonful of lard; knead well, and let it rise over night. In winter, let it begin to rise near the fire the first of the evening, unless your kitchen is very warm. But in summer do not mix until nine, unless you intend baking before breakfast. In the morning knead again, and make into loaves; let them rise one hour, and bake fifty minutes. If you have not plenty of milk, mix with water, and use one spoonful more of lard. There is a great deal in knowing how to knead; *strength* is not *all*, as many suppose. When you put the bread on the board, mix it lightly, and when you begin to knead it, do not *press down*, but let all your motions be as elastic as possible; knead with the palm of the hand until the dough is a flat cake, then *fold*, and keep doing this until the dough is smooth and elastic; twenty minutes is the time I have given, but many persons can knead the bread in less time, while others will require longer. But *practice* will teach each one.

Milk Yeast Bread.

Put into a two-quarts-and-a-pint pail one pint of *new* milk, and one pint of *boiling* water; mix with this one tablespoonful of white sugar, one of salt, and three pints of flour. Beat this well together, and cover tight (have a spoon that is so short that you can put the cover on the pail while it is in it, and yet it must be long enough to come nearly to the top.) Set this pail into another pail, or kettle, with water enough to come nearly to the top of it. To get this water the right temperature, take one half cold and one half boiling water; set it where it will keep about the same temperature until risen; watch carefully, and beat the batter as often as once in every half hour until the last hour, when it must not be disturbed. This will rise in about five hours; when it is risen the pail will be full. Do not let it stand one minute after that, as it spoils very quickly. Have in a pan two quarts of flour, make a hole in the middle of it. Dissolve a teaspoonful of saleratus in a little hot water, and when the batter is risen turn it into the middle of the flour, and turn the saleratus in with it; then knead well, and make into loaves. Set them where they will be warm, and let them rise forty-five minutes. Bake in a quick oven. It will take nearly a pint of flour to knead the dough on the board.

Be as particular to measure your flour as you are to measure the milk and water. This bread is not so healthful as hop yeast bread, and is more difficult to make; but it makes the nicest dry toast and delicious sandwiches.

Graham Bread.

Take two quarts of Graham (*never* sift it) and one of flour, half a cup of yeast, one scant spoonful of salt, half a cup of brown sugar, and warm water enough to make a stiff batter, and let it rise. If you rise it over night, be sure to set it in a cool place, as it sours much quicker than fine flour. It will rise in a warm place in four hours. When risen, mix with it a teaspoonful of saleratus dissolved in warm water, and flour enough to shape it into loaves; put it in the pans, and let it rise thirty-five minutes, and bake *slowly* an hour and a quarter. Make the loaves very small. Use molasses instead of sugar if the bread is eaten for constipation.

Third Bread.

Take one quart of flour, one of Indian meal, one of rye, one cup of yeast, one spoonful of salt, half a cup of brown sugar, and nearly a quart of warm water; mix well together, and let it rise over night. In the morning use flour enough to shape it into loaves, and let it rise in the baking-pans forty-five minutes. Bake one hour and a quarter.

Brown Bread.

Take one heaping pint bowlful of rye meal, two of Indian, one cup of yeast, one of molasses, one spoonful of salt, one teaspoonful saleratus. Mix with warm water, as thick as hasty pudding. Lard the dish in which it is to be baked, and then **turn** in the mixture; let it rise two hours, and bake in a slow oven four hours.

Brown Bread, No. 2.

Very nice. Three cups of Indian meal, three of rye, one half of molasses, one spoouful of salt, one teaspoonful of saleratus; wet with one quart and a fourth of milk. Steam five or six hours. This will make enough to fill a two quart pan.

Brown Bread, No. 3.

Nice. One pint of sour milk, half a cup of molasses, one teaspoonful saleratus, one tablespoonful salt, half Indian and half rye meal enough to make a stiff batter; lard the baking-tin well, and turn in the mixture. Steam five hours. I will say here that you cannot steam brown bread too much; but do not steam it less than five hours.

Raised Biscuit.

If the biscuit are for breakfast, take part of the dough of yeast bread No. 2, and mould with the hands *very small* cakes, place them in a shallow pan, and rise one hour. Bake in a quick oven thirty minutes. Never cut raised biscuit with a cutter; they are enough nicer for being moulded by the hand to pay for the extra labor. When the biscuit are for tea, take part of the dough of

No. 1, and proceed as directed for breakfast biscuit. When the supper hour is six, do not set your bread until ten, if in summer, but if in winter, half past eight. Begin to make the biscuit two hours before supper-time; by this means you will have plenty of time to rise them. Shape the loaves at the same time, and they can be baked while you are getting supper.

Raised Biscuit, No. 2.

Take three quarts of flour and one cup of butter, one of yeast, one spoonful of salt, one of sugar. Melt the butter and mix with a scant quart of warm milk; wet the flour with this, and set in a warm place to rise. When it cracks open it is risen enough. When it is risen, work into it two teaspoonfuls of saleratus which have been dissolved in half a cup of hot water. You must work it very thoroughly, or the saleratus will not be mixed with every part. Now put the dough into large tin pans or pails (do not have the vessels more than half full, as the dough will rise again), and set them on the ice. This dough will not be fit to use under twelve hours, as it must be chilled through. When you wish to make biscuit, take part of this dough and lay on the paste board, and roll about an inch thick; cut in small cakes, and bake fifteen minutes in a quick oven. Handle the dough as little as possible, and keep very cold until you put it in the oven This is a very nice way to make biscuit where the family have hot bread twice a day, as it will keep five days; but there must be a good ice-chest, and plenty of ice to have it work well.

White Mountain Rolls.

For breakfast. Sixteen cups of flour, one half a cup of white sugar, one cup of butter, one of yeast, the whites of four eggs beaten to a stiff froth, and four cups of boiled milk. Melt the butter, have the milk blood-warm, and mix the bread; set in a warm place, and rise over night; in the morning shape into long rolls rise one hour, and bake half an hour.

Parker House Rolls.

Take two quarts of flour, and rub into it a tablespoonful of lard and a little salt; put in a deep bread-pan, and make a hole in the flour, into which pour one pint of *cold boiled* milk and half a cup of yeast. Cover the pan, and let it stand all night; in the morning stir it up and knead well, and set in a warm place to rise; let it rise to a light sponge (it will rise in an hour a half), then roll it out on the board about half an inch thick; cut with an oval cutter, and fold about two thirds of it; lay them on tin sheets; let them rise an hour, and then bake in a quick oven fifteen minutes. If you have breakfast at seven, you must be up at four to have them ready.

Coffee Rolls.

Take twelve cups of flour, one of white sugar, one half of butter or lard, one of yeast, one grated nutmeg, and three eggs. Mix with three large cups of warm milk, and let it rise over night; if well risen in the morning, knead and set in a cool place until three o'clock in the afternoon, then shape into long rolls, as you do White Mountain rolls, and let them rise one hour and a half. Bake half an hour in a moderate oven. When done, glaze them with a little milk in which a little brown sugar has been dissolved, and set them back in the oven for two minutes. These are for tea. They are nice, sliced thin, when cold.

Bunns.

Bunns are made the same as coffee rolls, with the addition of two cups of English currants. They are shaped like biscuit, only a little smaller.

Soda Biscuit.

Take one quart of flour, before it is sifted, and put into the sieve, and with it one teaspoonful of saleratus, two of cream of tartar, one of salt, and one tablespoonful of white sugar. Mix all these thoroughly with the flour ; *then* run through the sieve, and then rub in one spoonful of lard or butter. Wet with a little over half a pint of milk. Roll on the board about an inch thick ; cut with a biscuit cutter, and bake in a quick oven fifteen minutes. If you have not milk, use a little more butter, and wet with water. Handle as little and make as rapidly as possible.

Cream of Tartar Rolls.

Take one pint of flour, before it is sifted, put into the sieve with one teaspoonful of cream of tartar, one half of saleratus, one half of salt, one of sugar, and mix them together, then run them through the sieve; wet with half a pint of milk. Heat and grease the French roll pan, and put a large spoonful into every compartment; set into a hot oven, and bake fifteen minutes. This quantity will make just one roll pan full.

Sour Milk Biscuit.

Rub half a spoonful of butter or lard into one quart of flour, and wet it with one quart of sour milk, into which you have previously stirred one teaspoonful of saleratus, which had been dissolved in a little hot water. Use as much more flour as you find necessary to make the dough stiff enough to roll out. Roll on the board about an inch thick and cut with a biscuit cutter. Bake in a quick oven. If you use lard for shortening, add one teaspoonful of salt.

Buttermilk Rolls.

Take two coffee cups of buttermilk, and stir into it one teaspoonful of saleratus dissolved in a little hot water, and stir into this about five cups of flour; beat this up lightly, and bake in French roll pans, the same as cream of tartar rolls. These are very nice. This will make two roll pans full.

Graham Rolls.

Take two coffee cups of sour milk, and stir into it one teaspoonful of saleratus, one of salt, half a cup of sugar, two eggs, one cup of flour, and Graham enough to make a stiff batter. Bake the same as cream of tartar rolls, allowing ten minutes longer.

Graham Rolls, No. 2.

Take one cup of *ice* water, half a teaspoonful of salt, and Graham enough to make a thick batter; beat this lightly, and bake in French roll pans in a quick oven. This makes one pan full.

Corn Rolls.

Corn rolls are made the same as Graham, using Indian meal instead of Graham.

Corn Cake.

Three teacups of Indian meal, one teaspoonful of salt, one tablespoonful of sugar, one of butter; wet this with *boiling* water, and then beat in one egg; spread half an inch deep on buttered tin sheets, and bake brown in a quick oven. This is delicious.

Corn Cake, No. 2.

Three teacupfuls of Indian meal, one of flour, one teaspoonful of salt, one tablespoonful of sugar, and one of yeast. Mix this with cold water enough to make a thin batter, let it rise over night, and in the morning add one teaspoonful of saleratus and one tablespoonful of melted butter. Bake in round tin plates in a quick oven.

Corn Cake, No. 3.

One pint of new milk, one pint of Indian meal, one pint of flour, half a cup of sugar, three eggs, one teaspoonful of saleratus, two of cream of tartar, salt. Measure the meal and flour after they have been sifted, and put into the sieve with the saleratus, cream of tartar, sugar, and salt. Mix well together and sift. Break the eggs into the pan in which you intend mixing the corn cake, and beat light; then turn in the milk and stir in the meal. Bake in tin plates in a quick oven.

Corn Cake, No. 4.

One pint of Indian meal, one handful of flour, half a cup of rice (measured before it is boiled) boiled soft, one quart of new milk, and a spoonful of salt. Boil the rice as directed for a vegetable, and drain dry (it may be boiled the night previous if you choose), and turn it into the milk; set the milk on in hot water, and let it boil, and when *boiling*, pour it on the meal and flour. Beat the eggs well and stir into the mixture. Turn it an inch deep into buttered pans, and bake thirty-five minutes. This can be made with or without the rice.

Rye Drop Cakes.

Three well-beaten eggs, one pint of new milk, one cup of flour, one teaspoonful of salt, one tablespoonful of sugar, and rye enough to make a stiff batter; half fill earthen cups, put them in an old pan (the one you use for baking potatoes), set in the oven, and bake one hour.

Flour Drop Cakes.

Flour drop cakes are made the same as rye, only do not have the batter so thick.

Flour Drop Cakes, No. 2.

One pint of new milk, four eggs, two tablespoonfuls of sugar, half a cup of butter, and four and a half of flour. Beat the eggs to a froth, melt the butter and turn upon the eggs with the milk and sugar; then stir in the flour, and bake in earthen cups one hour.

Graham Drop Cakes.

Graham drop cakes are made the same as rye, with the addition of half a cup of sugar.

Muffins.

One quart of milk, one cup of yeast, nine cups of flour, butter the size of a walnut, and four eggs. Make a batter with the milk, butter, yeast, and flour; beat the eggs and stir in; set in a warm place, and let it rise four hours, and then bake in buttered muffin rings, or fry on the griddle in rings.

Muffins, No. 2.

One pint of milk, one cup of sugar, five cups of flour, one teaspoonful of saleratus, two of cream of tartar, two eggs, and butter the size of an egg. Beat the butter and sugar together, and then add the eggs well beaten; with this mix the milk, and then beat in the flour in which the saleratus and cream of tartar have been mixed. Bake in buttered muffin rings in a quick oven.

Griddle Cakes.
Sour Milk or Buttermilk Cakes.

Two coffee cups of sour milk or buttermilk, one teaspoonful of saleratus dissolved in a little hot water, and flour enough to pour. Grease the griddle with a piece of fat salt pork, and fry the cakes a light brown.

Rice Cakes.

Make with sour milk, as directed above, and add two well-beaten eggs, one cup of boiled rice, and one teaspoonful of salt. They require a longer time to fry than the plain do, but are very nice.

Indian Cakes.

Make as the first, using half flour and half Indian meal, and one teaspoonful of salt. These require a longer time to fry than when made with all flour.

Corn Dodgers.

Take three teacups of Indian meal, one teaspoonful of salt, one tablespoonful of sugar, and pour on boiling water enough to wet it; then make into small flat cakes about an inch thick, and fry in *boiling* fat until brown. They will fry in fifteen or twenty minutes. To be eaten *very hot*.

Bread Cakes.

Take stale bread and soak it in milk; when soft, run it through a cullender. To one quart of this add one teaspoonful of saleratus, two eggs, one cup of flour, one teaspoonful of salt, two tablespoonfuls of sugar, and half a nutmeg. These also take some time to cook. The eggs may be omitted if you choose, but you must then use half a cup more of flour.

Buckwheat Cakes.

One pint of warm water, half a cup of yeast, one teaspoonful of salt, half a cup of Indian meal, two tablespoonfuls of molasses, and buckwheat enough to make a *thin* batter; let this rise over night; in the morning sift in one teaspoonful of saleratus, and fry. If you have them every morning, save a little of the batter to rise them with, instead of using fresh yeast every time. The Indian meal may be omitted if you prefer them without; in this case use a little more buckwheat. They may be made with sour milk, as the flour are made, by substituting buckwheat for flour; but they are not so good as when raised. Buckwheat is so fine that care must be taken to stir and beat well from the bottom, or there will be lumps of dry buckwheat there.

Fried Mush.

Into one quart of boiling water stir one tablespoonful of salt, and one cup of flour mixed with one quart of Indian meal (it may take a little more than a quart of meal to make it stiff enough); beat it well, or it will be lumpy. Boil gently two hours, and then turn into dishes which have been dipped in cold water, and set away to cool. Pans in which you bake loaves of bread are the best to cool it in, as it then makes handsome slices. In the morning cut into slices an inch thick, and fry brown in pork fat. Serve slices of fried pork with it. You can cook enough at one time for several breakfasts. If you do not wish to fry the mush, do not use the flour, and do not make quite so stiff.

Brown Bread Brewis.

If you bake brown bread there will be a great deal of hard crust. Take this crust and put in a basin with a little salt, and cold water enough to cover it; cover tight, and set on the fire to boil; boil fifteen or twenty minutes, and serve in a deep dish. It must be dry and soft. This is very nice eaten with cold corned beef or cold tongue; it can also be eaten with milk or sirup.

PLAIN CAKE.

Tea Cake.

ONE spoonful of butter, one cup of sugar, one of milk, one teaspoonful of saleratus, two of cream of tartar, and one pint of flour. Beat the sugar and butter together, and then the two eggs; next stir the milk with them, and then stir in the flour in which the saleratus and cream of tartar have been thoroughly mixed. Turn it, about an inch deep, into shallow pans, and bake in a quick oven. To be eaten warm.

Berry Cake.

Make the same as tea cake, only measure the pint of flour *before* it is sifted, and stir in one pint of blue berries.

Plain Cup Cake.

Half a cup of butter, one of sugar, three of flour, one of milk, three eggs, one teaspoonful of saleratus, two of cream of tartar, and lemon or nutmeg to taste. Beat the butter light, then add the sugar gradually, beating all the time until it is a cream, and then add the eggs, which have been beaten light, and the milk; mix all these well together, and then stir in the flour, in which the saleratus and cream of tartar have been mixed. Flavor and bake either in loaves or sheets; when done, the place on top where it has cracked open will look well done. If baked in loaves, it will take forty minutes; in sheets, twenty. This quantity will make two small loaves.

Richer Cup Cake.

One cup of butter, two of sugar, one of milk, four of flour, one teaspoonful of cream of tartar, half of saleratus, four eggs, and a nutmeg. Put together as directed for plain cup cake. This will make two large loaves. Bake in a moderate oven fifty minutes, or more.

Railroad Cake.

One cup of sugar, one half of milk, one and a half of flour, two tablespoonfuls of butter, two eggs, one teaspoonful of cream of tartar, and one half of saleratus. Flavor with lemon, and bake in thin sheets Put together as directed for plain cup cake.

Cream Cake.

Very nice. Beat to a froth one cup of sugar and three eggs, and on this pour one cup of sweet cream; then stir in one and a half cups of flour in which one teaspoonful of saleratus and two of cream of tartar are thoroughly mixed. Flavor with lemon, and pour into shallow pans Bake, in a rather quick oven, thirty minutes.

Feather Cake.

One cup of sugar, one of milk, two scant cups of flour, one egg, one tablespoonful of butter, half a tea spoonful of saleratus, one of cream of tartar, and flavor to taste. Soften (but do not *melt*) the butter, and beat it with the sugar and egg; then add the milk, and then the flour mixed with the saleratus and cream of tartar. Bake in shallow pans in a quick oven.

Sponge Cake.

Three eggs, one and a half cups of sugar, two of flour, one half of cold water, one teaspoonful of cream of tartar, one half of saleratus. Beat the sugar and eggs together, and add the water when they are light, then the flour, in which mix the saleratus and cream of tartar. Flavor with lemon, and bake in a quick oven.

Sponge Cake, No. 2.

One cup of sugar, three eggs, one cup of flour, one teaspoonful of cream of tartar, and half of saleratus. Beat sugar and eggs together, and then beat in the flour in which the saleratus is mixed. Flavor with lemon, and bake in sheets in a quick oven.

Allie's Cake.

One cup of molasses, one of sugar, one of sour milk, three of flour, one half of butter, one pound of raisins, one teaspoonful of saleratus, two of cinnamon, and one of cloves. Beat sugar and butter together, then add molasses and spice, then the sour milk in which the saleratus is dissolved, and then the flour, and last the raisins. Bake in loaves in a moderate oven. If the raisins are not stoned, chop them. It is much better, however, to stone them.

Raisin Cake.

One cup of molasses, one of butter, one of milk, three of flour, two of chopped raisins, and one teaspoonful of saleratus. Spice to your taste. Soften the butter and beat it and the molasses together; then add milk, and then the flour in which the saleratus is mixed, and lastly the raisins. Bake in loaves in a moderate oven.

Apple Cake.

Wash clean two cups of sliced dried apple, and soak over night; in the morning chop one half of them, and stew them all slowly in two cups of molasses, until they are dark. One cup of butter, two of sugar, two of chopped raisins, two thirds of sour milk, four eggs, two teaspoonfuls of saleratus, five cups of flour, and all kinds of spice. Put together as directed for raisin cake, and stir in the apple and raisins last. Bake in loaves, in a moderate oven, from two hours and a half to three.

Rich Molasses Gingerbread.

Two cups of molasses, two of milk, one of melted butter, two and a half teaspoonfuls of saleratus, three eggs, one tablespoonful of ginger, and one nutmeg, one cup of sugar, and eight cups of flour. Beat molasses, butter, sugar, and eggs together; then dissolve the saleratus in the milk, and add it with flour, ginger, and nutmeg; beat up well, and pour about two inches deep into pans, and bake half an hour. This will keep well, but being nearly as expensive as cup cake, I would rather make it plainer and oftener.

Soft Molasses Gingerbread, No. 2.

One cup of molasses, one teaspoonful of saleratus, one of ginger, one tablespoonful of butter or lard, a pinch of salt, if you use lard. Stir this together, and then pour on one half a cup of *boiling* water, one pint of flour. Bake about one inch deep in a sheet. This is very nice if pains are taken to have the water boiling, and to beat it well when the flour is added.

Soft Molasses Gingerbread, No. 3.

One cup of molasses, one of sugar, one of sour milk, one tablespoonful of ginger, half of saleratus, one egg, and flour enough to make a thick batter. Bake about one inch deep in a tin sheet.

Hard Molasses Gingerbread.

One pint of molasses, half a cup of lard or butter, (half a tablespoonful of salt when you use lard), one tablespoonful of ginger, one of saleratus; beat all this together, and when well mixed add half a pint of *cold* water, and flour enough to roll. Roll this very *thin* and cut in strips about three inches wide and six long, with a jagging-iron, and bake in a quick oven until brown. When you take them from the oven, lay them on a sieve to cool, and when cold, put them in a tin box that can be covered tight; keep this in a dry closet, and they will keep nice and crispy for a month.

Hard Sugar Gingerbread.

One cup of butter, two of sugar, one of sour milk, two eggs, one tablespoonful of ginger, one teaspoonful of saleratus, and flour enough to roll. Beat the sugar and butter to a cream, then beat in the eggs, ; add the ginger and sour milk in which the saleratus is dissolved, and then the flour. Roll about half an inch thick; cut, bake, and keep the same as directed for hard molasses gingerbread.

Ginger Snaps.

One cup of molasses, one of butter, one of sugar, one tablespoonful of ginger, and two eggs. Put the molasses and butter in a tin pan, and set one the fire; when it boils up, take off, and add the sugar and ginger.

When they are well mixed, add the eggs, which have been well beaten, and then flour enough to roll. Put a small piece at a time on the board, and roll as thin as the blade of a knife; cut into round cakes, and bake in a quick oven until they are a dark brown. Cool, and keep in a tin box, the same as hard gingerbread.

Molasses Cookies.

One cup of molasses, one of brown sugar, one of lard, one half of boiling water, one spoonful of ginger, one of saleratus, one of salt, and flour enough to roll. Beat sugar, lard, molasses, saleratus, and ginger together; then pour on the boiling water, and mix in the flour. Roll about three quarters of an inch thick, and cut with a round cutter. Bake in a quick oven.

Vinegar Cookies.

Two cups of molasses, one of butter or lard, two eggs, two tablespoonfuls of vinegar, one of ginger, one of saleratus, and flour enough to roll. Roll about half an inch thick, cut into round cakes, and bake in a quick oven.

Sugar Cookies.

One cup of sugar, half a cup of butter, one cup of milk, two eggs, half a nutmeg, one teaspoonful saleratus, and flour enough to roll. Beat sugar and butter to a cream, then add the eggs, well beaten, dissolve the saleratus in the milk, and stir that in, then the flour.

Jumbles.

Three cups of sugar, two of butter, three eggs, one teaspoonful of saleratus, four tablespoonfuls of sour cream, and flour enough to roll. Beat sugar and butter to a cream, then add the eggs, which are well beaten, then the sour cream in which the saleratus is dissolved. Flavor with anything you please. Cut with an oval cutter. If you have a cutter that takes a piece out of the centre, use that. When you roll them, sift over the dough, before you cut it, granulated sugar, and then roll the pin lightly over it. This is a much better way than to sift the sugar on after the cakes are put in the pan, for when sifted in the pan it burns on it, and spoils the looks of the pan and cakes. Great care must be taken in baking all kinds of cakes which you roll on the board, as they burn very quickly; and again, if they are not baked enough, they will not be nice, keep well, or be healthful. Where there are children, this is the most economical way to make cake, but takes more time; and also in families where they do not care for cake, they are nice to keep in case of unexpected company.

Plain Doughnuts.

One pint of flour, half a cup of sugar, one spoonful of butter, one teaspoonful of cream of tartar, one half of saleratus, half a nutmeg, and milk enough to wet and roll. Soften the butter and mix with the milk (about one cupful); mix the sugar, saleratus, cream of tartar, and the nutmeg with the flour, and stir into the butter and milk. After beating well with the spoon, put on the board, roll about an inch thick, and cut in any shape you please. Have ready *boiling* lard or drippings, and fry until done, which will be in about eight minutes. The addition of two eggs is an improvement, but not necessary. When you have finished frying, cut a potato in slices and put in the fat to clarify it, then set the kettle one side until it settles, then strain into an earthen pot (keep one on purpose for this), and set in a cool place. The sediments which remain in the bottom put in the soap-grease. Many persons fry doughnuts in the common frying-pan, but there is not depth enough to it. It is much better, if you have not an iron kettle that is deep enough, to use a tin basin.

Raised Doughnuts.

One cup of sweet milk, one spoonful of butter, four of yeast, four of sugar, half a nutmeg, and flour to make a stiff batter; let this rise over night. In the morning roll out, cut in strips, with a jagging-iron, about four inches long and two wide, and fry. Common raised dough makes very nice ones to be eaten as soon as fried, either for breakfast or tea.

Doughnuts should not be eaten before November or after April; indeed, they are not very healthful to eat at any time. Keep covered in a stone pot in the cellar.

PUDDINGS.

Boiled Rice.

PICK and wash clean one cupful of rice, and put into a basin with a pint and a half of cold water; set on the stove where it will cook slowly; or, better still, set into another basin of water, and cook slowly. When the rice has absorbed all the water, turn on it one quart of new milk, and stir in one tablespoonful of salt; let this cook two hours, stirring often. Serve with sugar and cream

Boiled Rice, No. 2.

Pick and wash one cup of rice, and boil in one quart of boiling water fifteen minutes, and then drain dry. Wring a pudding-cloth out of boiling water, and spread in a deep dish, and turn the rice into it, and sprinkle in one cup of raisins and a tablespoonful of salt; tie the cloth loosely that the rice may have room to swell, and boil two hours Serve with lemon sauce, or sugar and cream.

Baked Rice.

Boil half a cup of rice in one pint of water thirty minutes, and then add one quart of new milk, and boil thirty minutes longer; then beat together one cup of sugar, three eggs, two teaspoonfuls of salt, and a little lemon or nutmeg; stir this into the rice and turn the mixture into a buttered pudding-dish, and bake thirty minutes. To be eaten without sauce.

Baked Rice, No. 2.

Pick and wash one cup of rice; put it in a dish that will hold two quarts and a pint, and cover with fresh milk; stir into this two teaspoonfuls of salt, one tablespoonful of cinnamon, and four of sugar. Set this in the oven, and stir once in every half hour; after it has been baking two hours stir in milk enough to fill the dish, and bake one hour longer (the dish should be nearly full of milk at first). Serve with sugar and milk.

Minute Pudding.

One pint of milk, one of water, nine tablespoonfuls of flour, one teaspoonful of salt, two eggs. Set the milk into a basin of hot water, and when it comes to a boil add to it one pint of boiling water. Have ready the flour, made into a smooth paste with one cup of milk, and mix with this paste, after they are well beaten, the two eggs; now take the basin in which the milk and water are, and set upon the fire; let it boil up once, and then stir in the thickening; beat it well, that it may be smooth, and cook three minutes longer. Serve with vinegar sauce.

Corn Starch Pudding.

One quart of milk, six tablespoonfuls of corn starch, three eggs, one teaspoonful of salt. Put the milk in a basin, and set the basin into a kettle with boiling water, and when it comes to a boil stir in the corn starch and eggs, which prepare in the following manner: Wet the corn starch with one cup of cold milk, and then stir into it the eggs which are well beaten. After the starch is added to the boiling milk it will cook in three minutes: beat well to make smooth. Serve with sugar and cream or wine sauce. Never add the eggs after the starch has been stirred into the boiling milk; if you do the egg will be in spots in it.

Quaking Pudding.

Take as much stale bread as will fill a quart basin after it is cut; now butter well a tin mould or pail that will cover tight, and put in a layer of bread; then strew in a few raisins, and then bread, and so on until the bread is all used (the bread must be cut very *thin*). Make a custard of three pints of milk and six eggs, and season with salt and nutmeg; turn this on the bread, and set away in a cool place two hours, and then set in a steamer and steam three. Serve with wine sauce. This may be boiled in a pudding-cloth. When boiled, prepare the same as for steaming, omitting the buttering of the dish, and let it soak two hours and a half, then turn into the pudding-cloth, tie tight, and boil two hours and a half.

Bride's Pudding.

Make the same as plain corn starch pudding, using the yolks of six eggs. Butter a pudding-dish, and turn the pudding into it (do not fill within three inches of the top of the dish), and bake thirty minutes; then take from the oven, and let it stand in a cool place twenty minutes; then cover with a meringue. Set in the oven ten minutes, and serve with cold sauce. To make the meringue, beat the whites of the eggs to a stiff froth, and then beat into them gradually one cup of sugar. This pudding is quite nice made with four eggs, but will not look so handsome

Bread Pudding.

Take a quart basinful of stale bread, and soak in two quarts of sweet milk two hours (keep in a cool place while soaking); then mash well with a spoon, and take out all the hard pieces. Beat light four eggs and stir into this, then add two teaspoonfuls of salt, a little nutmeg, and one fourth of a cup of sugar, if you serve it with sauce; if not, one and a half cupfuls. Bake three quarters of an hour, and serve with lemon sauce. Some put raisins in, but it must be much stiffer if you have them, and the delicacy of the pudding is thereby lost.

Whortleberry Pudding.

One cup of butter, two of sugar, one of sour milk, four of flour, five eggs, one teaspoonful of saleratus, and one quart of berries Beat the sugar and butter to a cream and add the eggs well beaten; then the sour milk, in which the saleratus is dissolved, and then the flour, and lastly the berries. Wring the pudding-cloth out of boiling water and spread it in a deep dish; then turn the batter in and tie. Have ready a kettle of boiling water, and drop the pudding into it; turn the pudding often, and boil three hours. Serve with vinegar or wine sauce. This can be steamed also. Allow half an hour longer to cook, when steamed.

Plain Whortleberry Pudding.

One pint of flour, one egg, half a pint of sweet milk, one teaspoonful of cream tartar, half of saleratus, and a quart of berries. Beat the egg to a froth and mix with the milk; then stir in the flour, in which the saleratus and cream tartar are thoroughly mixed; then the berries. Boil and serve as directed above.

Boiled Apple Pudding.

Pare, boil, and mash six good-sized mealy potatoes, and turn on them half a pint of boiling milk, then stir in a teaspoonful of salt and a tablespoonful of butter; set in a cool place, and stir until about blood warm; then stir in flour enough to roll, and roll about an inch thick. Have a two-quart basinful of apples, which are pared, cored, and quartered; spread these on the paste and grate a little nutmeg over them; then roll up the paste, and boil as directed for berry pudding, and serve with either maple sirup, wine, or vinegar sauce. This can be steamed, allowing four hours for it to cook.

Boiled Batter Pudding.

Take one cup of flour, and add to it gradually one quart of sweet milk; then stir in one teaspoonful of salt and six well-beaten eggs. Turn this into the pudding-cloth, and tie tight, leaving room for it to swell one third. Boil two hours. Serve with wine sauce. Great care must be taken in boiling puddings to have the water *boiling when you put the pudding in*, and to *keep it boiling all the time*. Steaming is the safer way, and I would always steam rather than boil, if I had the convenience. When boiling, always keep a kettle of boiling water to fill up, as it boils away from the pudding. For a pudding-cloth get three quarters of a yard of drilling. Keep an old saucer to put in the bottom of the kettle, in which you boil the pudding, to prevent its being burned. When you are ready to dish the pudding, have a pan of cold water, into which plunge it immediately upon taking it from the kettle (but do not let it stand in cold water one second); then put it in a deep dish, and untie the string; open the cloth and turn the pudding-dish on it; then lift the pudding up by means of the cloth, and turn over. You will thus preserve the shape of the pudding. Batter puddings are very difficult to make, and I would not advise a young cook to try them at first.

Baked Apple Pudding.

Make a paste as directed for plain pie-crust, and line a dish with it, and fill the dish with sliced apples. To a dish holding three quarts, allow one cup of sugar, one half of molasses, one of water, one nutmeg, and half a teaspoon of cinnamon; cover this with the paste, and bake slowly three hours. Serve with sugar and cream, or with cold sauce.

Pan Dowdy.

Pare and slice tart apples enough to fill, about two inches deep, a flat earthen or tin pan. To three quarts of apple add one cup of sugar, one grated nutmeg, one cup of cold water, and butter the size of a walnut. Cover this with plain pie-crust (have the crust about an inch thick), and bake slowly two hours and a half; then cover and set where it will keep *hot* one hour. Serve with sugar and cream. When done the apple will look red. Do not break the crust into the apple after baking, as by this means you spoil the pastry. If you wish to have it richer, cover with puff paste.

Apple Dowdy.

Pare and quarter about one dozen good tart apples, put them in a kettle with one cup of molasses, a small piece of butter, and one pint of hot water. Set this on the fire, and let it come to a boil, and while it is heating make a paste with one pint of flour, one teaspoon of cream tartar, one half of saleratus, and a little milk; roll this large enough to fit into the kettle, and when the mixture begins to boil, put the paste in, cover tight, and boil gently twenty minutes. To be eaten without sauce. This is very nice when the apples are tart and it is made well

Apple Charlotte.

Butter a brown earthen dish, and place around the sides slices of bread which have been cut about an inch thick, soaked in cold water, and buttered; fill the dish with sliced apples, and grate over them one nutmeg; strew on one cup of sugar, and then pour on one cup of water; this will carry the sugar through the apple. Cover the apple with slices of soaked and buttered bread, then cover the whole with a large plate, and bake in a very moderate oven four hours. Remove from the oven half an hour before time to dish, and set where it will be cooling. When ready to dish, loosen gently round the edges with a knife, lay the dish in which you intend serving it on the one in which it was baked, turn the dishes over, and lift the pudding-dish off. This is a very handsome dish. Serve with sugar and cream or plain.

Apple and Sago Pudding.

Wash half a cup of sago, and set on the fire with three pints of cold water; simmer two hours; then stir in one cup of white sugar, one teaspoonful of salt, and one of the extract of lemon. Have ready a deep pudding-dish, in which, after it has been well buttered, put as many pared and cored apples as will stand in the dish; turn over them the sago, and bake one hour in a moderate oven. Serve with sugar and cream.

Tapioca and Apple Pudding.

Prepare the tapioca as directed for sago. Pare and quarter ten tart apples, and when the tapioca is cooked stir them into it, turn them into a buttered pudding-dish, and bake one hour and a quarter. Remove the pudding from the oven half an hour before it is served, or it will be thin. Serve with sugar and cream.

Boiled Tapioca Pudding.

Wash one cup of tapioca, and soak it one hour in one pint of cold water, then stir in one quart of milk and two teaspoonfuls of salt; set the basin into another of hot water, and set on the fire; cook one hour and a half. Serve with sugar and cream.

Baked Tapioca Pudding.

Prepare the tapioca as before directed, allowing one pint more of milk for the same quantity of tapioca. Beat together one cup of sugar and four eggs; stir this into the tapioca, and flavor with lemon or nutmeg. Bake in a buttered dish half an hour. Serve without sauce, or omit the sugar and serve with wine sauce.

Custard Pudding.

Beat together three tablespoonfuls of sugar and four eggs; stir this into one quart of milk, with one teaspoonful of salt; flavor with nutmeg or lemon. Bake until firm in the centre; this you tell by inserting the handle of a teaspoon. Do not let the oven get hot enough to *boil* it.

Baked Indian Pudding.

Three tablespoonfuls of Indian meal, one cup of molasses, two quarts of milk, two eggs, butter half the size of an egg, one tablespoonful of ginger, two teaspoonfuls of salt; boil one quart of the milk, and pour it boiling on the meal, then turn in the molasses, and next the cold milk, butter, ginger, salt, and eggs. Bake five hours in a moderate oven. Serve with cream. The eggs and ginger may be omitted if you choose.

Cottage Pudding.

One spoonful of butter, one cup of sugar, one cup of milk, one pint of flour, two eggs, one teaspoonful of saleratus, two of cream of tartar. Soften the butter, and then beat to a froth with the sugar and eggs; then add the milk, and lastly the flour, in which the saleratus and cream of tartar are thoroughly mixed. Flavor with lemon, and bake in two shallow pudding-dishes half an hour, in a moderate oven. Serve with lemon sauce. The pudding is improved by sifting sugar over it, before baking.

Sponge Pudding.

Beat to a froth three eggs and one cup of sugar; stir into this half a cup of cold water, and then two cups of flour in which are mixed one teaspoonful of saleratus and two of cream of tartar. Flavor with lemon, and bake in two shallow dishes. When baked frost with frosting No. 2, and let it stand in a warm place ten minutes, then send to the table with lemon sauce. Bake twenty-five minutes.

Italian Fritters.

Cut stale bread into slices an inch thick, and soak them in a custard made with two eggs and a pint of milk; then fry a light brown in boiling lard (have as much lard in the pan as you would for doughnuts), and serve with either wine sauce No. 2 or cider sauce. Have the dishes very hot.

I have here given rules for twenty-three plain puddings, and if anything richer is desired, it will be found in Part Second.

PIES.

Plain Pie Crust.

INTO one quart of flour rub a large spoonful of salt and half a cup of lard, and then wet with ice-water enough to make a soft paste; roll this on the board until it is about half an inch thick, then spread on half a cup of washed butter, dredge with flour, and fold into a small square. Pound lightly with the rolling-pin, then roll out again; roll it up, and set on the ice to harden; it will be ready to use in two hours. In winter it can be used immediately. To make the bottom crust, rub three quarters of a cup of lard into one quart of flour and one spoonful of salt, and wet with cold water, to make a soft paste. Do not roll, as it makes it tough Butter is more healthful than lard; therefore, if you can afford it, use it.

Cream Paste.

To one quart of flour add one spoonful of salt, and mix to a soft paste with sweet cream; roll thin and spread with cream and dredge with flour, fold and roll again; repeat this operation three times, then make the pies. Pies made with this paste taste nice, and are not hurtful, but do not look so handsome as when made with butter and lard. Look in Part Second for minute direction for making paste.

Sliced Apple Pies.

Line the plates with bottom crust, and fill the plate with quartered apples. To a common-sized plate allow two spoonfuls of sugar, a little nutmeg, and two spoonfuls of water. Cut the upper crust a little larger than the plate, and raise the under crust with the blade of the knife, and lay it under it. Bake in a moderate oven one hour. When molasses is preferred, use three spoonfuls, and a little cinnamon instead of nutmeg.

Stewed Apple Pies.

Pare, core, and stew the apples with just water enough to prevent their burning. To a quart of stewed apple allow one cup of sugar. Bottom the plates and roll a piece of the top crust out (making it long enough to go around the plate), cut into strips an inch wide, and lay around the plate, then put in the apple (Do not make the pie too thick.) Grate over it a little nutmeg, cover, and bake in a rather quick oven forty minutes.

Dried Apple Pies.

Cook the apple according to the directions given in Part Second, under Dried Apple, and make the same as stewed apple pie.

Berry Pies.

Line the plates, and fill as full as you can with berries, and dredge on about half a spoonful of flour, and two spoonfuls of sugar, and two of water; cover as directed for sliced apple pies, and bake forty minutes in a moderate oven. All berry pies are made in this manner, if they are very sour using more sugar. Cherries and currants do not require any water, but more sugar, and they must not be heaped in the plate as blueberries, blackberries, raspberries, and strawberries are.

Rhubarb Pies.

Cut the rhubarb in the morning, or if you buy it, always keep in a cool place until ready to cook it. Strip off the skin and cut it into pieces about an inch long; stew in just water enough to prevent its burning; when cold, sweeten to taste. Cover the pie-plates, and roll the upper crust about half an inch thick; cut into strips an inch wide, and after filling the plate with the rhubarb, put on four cross-pieces and the rim. Bake half an hour.

Squash Pies.

Pare, boil, and sift a good dry squash. To one quart of the squash pour on two of boiling milk, and then stir in two cups of sugar, two spoonfuls of salt, one of cinnamon, one grated nutmeg, and five well-beaten eggs. Line deep plates with plain paste, fill with the mixture, and bake one hour in a moderate oven. The pies look nice to boil a stick of cinnamon in the milk, instead of using the ground.

Cranberry Pies.

Stew the cranberries according to directions in Part Second, and make the same as rhubarb pies.

Gooseberry Pies.

Stew the gooseberries in as little water as possible, sweeten to taste, and make the same as rhubarb pies.

Pumpkin Pies.

Pare and cut the pumpkin into small pieces; wash and put into the kettle with one quart of water; boil six hours, stirring often to prevent burning; then run it through a sieve. Make the same as squash, adding a teaspoonful of ginger. They may be made without eggs by using five pounded crackers. Cook enough of the pumpkin at a time to last two weeks; after you have kept it one week, set in the oven and scald, then set away in a cool place.

Custard Pies.

Line a deep plate with paste; make the custard the same as for custard pudding; fill the plate, and bake until firm in the centre.

Mince Pies.

Boil a shank of beef six hours; then take up and set away to cool. (Save the liquor for soup.) When cold, free from bones and cut off all the fat and gristle; then chop fine. To one quart of the chopped meat add three of chopped apple, one pint of chopped suet, one quart of chopped raisins, one quart of sugar, one of molasses, half a cup of cinnamon, one quarter of a cup of cloves, one quarter of a cup of allspice, one quarter of a cup of ground mace, six grated nutmegs, half a cup of salt. Mix this *thoroughly* with the *hands*, then turn on the mixture three quarts of good cider, and let the mixture stand over night. In the morning scald, in a porcelain kettle, one hour; then put in stone pots; cover tight and keep in a cool, dry place. This will keep three months. To tell the exact amount of spice and sweetening is almost impossible, as tastes vary; but with a little judgment, and the rule I have given, I think there cannot be any very serious trouble. Prepare the paste and plates as for stewed apple pies, and put in the meat; then grate a little nutmeg over it, and strew a few whole raisins in; cover and bake one hour in a moderate oven.

Mock Mince Pies.

Two pounded crackers, one cup of molasses, one of cider, one of chopped raisins, two eggs, one teaspoonful of salt, one of clove, two of cinnamon, one of mace, one nutmeg. Bake forty minutes. This quantity makes two pies.

Lemon Pies.

Soak a pounded cracker in one pint of new milk; stir in to this the yolks of three and the whites of two eggs, which have been beaten with half a cup of sugar and the rind and juice of one lemon Bake in a deep plate, which has been lined with plain paste, half an hour. When cooked, beat the white of one egg to a froth, and stir in one spoonful of sugar; set in the oven until a light brown.

Cream Pies.

Three eggs beaten with one and a half cups of sugar, half a cup of cold water, two cups of flour in which are mixed one half teaspoonful of saleratus, one of cream of tartar. Flavor with lemon. Bake in deep tin plates such as you use for squash-pies, and when cool split with a sharp knife, and fill. This will make four pies.

Filling for Cream Pies.

One pint of new milk, one cup of sugar, half a cup of flour, two eggs. Put the basin, in which the milk is, into another of hot water. Beat the sugar, flour, and eggs together until they are light and smooth, and when the milk boils, stir in with one teaspoonful of salt. Cook twenty minutes, stirring often. Flavor with lemon. This will fill four pies.

PIES. 115

Washington Pies.

Make the outside the same as for cream pies, and fill with any kind of jelly or jam you choose. For richer pies look in Part Second.

Remarks.

Always measure flour after it has been sifted, unless told to measure before. Always sift Indian and rye meal, and never sift Graham or oat meal. Always set milk into boiling water to boil, as it boils quicker in this way, and there will be no danger of burning. Save all the fat from soups, boiled and roast meats. The fat from beef, pork, and poultry, keep for shortening or frying; and from ham, mutton, and soups, in which vegetable were boiled, for the soap grease. To clarify drippings, boil them a few minutes, and then cut in a raw potato, and let it cook for five minutes, then drop in a pinch of saleratus, and strain. If all the drippings are taken care of, it will be a great saving in a family. In many of the rules given here it has been very difficult to say just how much spice to use, as there is such a difference in tastes, so that each one must use her own judgment; but be careful that one spice predominates. Always use twice as much cinnamon and nutmeg as you do clove. In making frosting, pudding sauce, and all kinds of delicate cake, use the powdered sugar, if possible. For rich cake, the coffee-crushed, powdered and sifted, is the best. For dark cake, the brown sugar will be found the nicest. It makes it richer. Save all the pieces of bread for dressing, puddings, and griddle cakes. Tin is not very good to mix cake in, and earthen dishes are always being broken. The stone china wash bowls are very good for this purpose. You can often find odd ones at the crockery stores, and they will last a lifetime for this purpose. In baking and frying cook everything *brown*. Bread and pastry are more healthful over-done, than under-done.

One even quart of sifted flour is one pound, one pint of granulated sugar is one pound, two good-sized cups of butter are one pound. Do not buy large quantities of Indian and rye meal at a time, as they sour quickly. Keep all kinds of meal, flour, and meats in a cool, dry place. Keep tea, coffee, and extracts from the air. Never set anything into the ice-chest while warm, as it will heat the chest and absorb an unpleasant flavor from the chest. This is true of the cellar also. Keep a note-book for tried receipts, and for any changes which you wish to make in the receipts which you are constantly using. By thought and observation one can learn something new in regard to cooking every day, and at the time it will seem so important that you cannot forget it; but you will if you do not have it written.

In the miscellaneous receipts will be found some very nice ones for the family table. They are receipts which I forgot, or did not receive until after the book was all written and classified. But they were too valuable to be left out, and I therefore put them in under this heading.

THE APPLEDORE COOK BOOK.

PART SECOND.

SOUPS.

Soup Stock.

IF you buy fresh meat for a soup stock, the shank is the most economical. Have it cut into several pieces, and the bone cracked, at the butcher's. Wash and put on to boil in two gallons of cold water, and one spoonful of salt (the salt helps the scum to rise). When it comes to a boil, take off the scum and set the kettle where the soup will just simmer for ten hours. Then strain into a nice tin, which is kept for this purpose, or a stone pot; set where it will be cold, and in the morning skim off all the fat, then turn gently into the soup-kettle, being careful not to turn in the sediment. It is now ready to make any kind of soup. If you wish to have a jelly in the morning, boil it in six quarts of water. You can then, after taking off the fat, turn the jelly over, and scrape off the sediment. Use the meat for hash. Another way to make soup stock, is to cover the bones of roast meats with cold water and treat in the same manner. This should always be done in boarding-houses and hotels; but in private families (unless very large), there is not meat enough consumed to do this. When making a stock, however, if there are any cold meat bones, they should be used. Professor Blot does not recommend boiling; but I have been more successful in obtaining *clear* soup in this manner than when I did not let it boil. I would always boil my stock the day before it is to be used, as by this means only can fat be avoided, unless you buy all lean beef, which is very expensive. Do not boil vegetables with the stock, as they cause it to sour quickly.

Brown Soup.

Crack the bone of a shank of beef; take out the marrow and lay in the bottom of the soup-kettle; cut the meat from the bones and lay it in the kettle, set the kettle on the fire and brown the meat on all sides, being careful not to burn it. When well browned, put in the bones and two quarts of cold water, cover tight, and let it simmer one hour; then put in a stick of cinnamon, eight whole cloves, a few pieces of mace, one onion, one carrot, half a turnip and six quarts of water. Boil this six hours very gently, strain and set away. In the morning skim off the fat and turn the soup into the kettle; let it come to a boil; season to taste with pepper and salt; cut in thin slices one fresh lemon and put into the soup, and then turn into the tureen. Send to table toasted bread, cut into small squares, in a separate dish. Some think that half a wine-glass of brandy is an improvement.

Brown Soup, No. 2.

Lay the bones from a roast of beef and a roast of mutton in the soup-kettle. Cut up one onion, one small turnip, one carrot, one parsnip, and lay in the kettle; then a blade of mace, a stick of cinnamon, ten whole cloves, a sprig of parsley, a sprig of sage, if you have them green, if not, a teaspoonful of each; now dredge in a cup of flour, a tablespoonful of salt, half of pepper; then pour on eight quarts of cold water, and boil five hours (skim carefully when it first boils); then strain through a sieve, and put back into the kettle with one cup of sago, and boil one hour and a half. Serve with toasted bread. Any kind of bones will make this, but beef is the best.

Brown Soup, No. 3.

Take two quarts of stock and boil with one onion, one carrot, one turnip, six whole cloves, one blade of mace, one stick of cinnamon, for one hour; then strain into the tureen, and serve with toasted bread.

Vegetable Soup.

Cut into strips two inches long and one fourth of an inch wide, two carrots, two parsnips, one turnip, and a very small piece of cabbage. Cover these with water and boil one hour; then strain them and put in the soup-kettle with three quarts of stock; let this boil up once. Season with pepper and salt, and serve.

Julienne Soup.

This is made the same as vegetable soup, putting in every kind of a green vegetable. It is made in June, July, and the first of August. The stock should be very clear. (Omit beets.)

Barley Soup.

Wash half a cup of pearl barley, and boil it slowly in one quart of water three hours; then turn into the soup kettle, with three quarts of stock; let this boil up and season with pepper and salt. Serve.

Sago Soup.

Make the same as barley, using sago. Two hours will cook it.

Macaroni Soup.

Made in the same way.

Vermicelli Soup.

Made in the same way.

Ox-Tail Soup.

Separate at the joints two ox-tails, put them on to boil with one onion, one carrot (have them whole), a few cloves, a blade of mace, and a stick of cinnamon. Boil two hours; then strain the liquor, into the soup-kettle, separate the tails from the vegetables, and spice, and put them into the kettle; to this add two quarts of stock; season with pepper and salt; boil up once, and serve.

Tomato Soup.

Peel and slice tomatoes enough to fill a two-quart basin; put them into the soup-kettle with six quarts of water and two pounds of beef; boil three hours; season with pepper, salt, and a spoonful of butter. Strain, and serve with toasted bread.

Giblet Soup.

Boil the giblets of six fowls in three quarts of water. with one onion, one carrot, one small turnip, one parsnip, a few cloves, a blade of mace, a stick of cinnamon, and two heaping spoonfuls of flour, for two hours; then strain into the soup kettle. Add to this two quarts of stock, and let it boil. Braid up the livers, chop the hearts and gizzards, and put them in the soup. Season with salt and pepper, and serve.

Turkey Soup.

Save the liquor in which the turkey was cooked; the

following morning skim of all the fat; cut all the meat from the part of the turkey which has been left from the dinner of the day previous. Put the bones and liquor on to boil with one onion, two parsnips, one small turnip. Boil three hours; then strain, and put back with half a cup of tapioca, and some pieces of the cold turkey. Season with pepper and salt. Boil two hours longer, stirring often to prevent the tapioca from burning.

Chicken Soup.

Set the liquor, in which two or three fowls have been boiled, away to cool. Skim off the fat, and then put it into the soup-kettle with one whole onion and half a cup of rice; boil two hours. Just before dishing take out the onion, and put in some pieces of cold chicken.

White Soup.

Take any part of veal (the shin is the best), and allow one quart of cold water to one pound of veal, and to eight pounds allow one onion, three parsnips, one turnip, a stick of cinnamon, and a blade of mace. Boil five hours, and season with salt and white pepper. when it has boiled four hours, thicken with two cups of flour. Boil one hour longer; strain, and serve.

Beef Soup.

Boil six pounds of beef in seven quarts of water, with one onion, one carrot, one turnip, and eight whole

SOUPS.   123

cloves, for six hours; strain, and thicken with half a cup of flour, and boil one hour longer, then stir in some of the beef cut into small pieces, and serve.

N. B. Use celery in all kinds of soup when you can obtain it.

Mock Turtle Soup.

Take the brains from a calf's head, and put them in a bowl of cold water; wash the head, and let it stand in a pan of cold water two hours; then put it in the soup-kettle with eight quarts of cold water and a shin of veal; let this boil three hours, and then set away to cool over night. In the morning cut up the veal and put into the soup-kettle, with a stalk of celery, one onion, one carrot, one turnip, two parsnips, three blades of mace, one stick of cinnamon, ten cloves, salt, pepper, and two heads of parsley. Cover this with three pints of cold water, and boil two hours. Strain this, and wash the soup-kettle, then turn the soup back. Now skim the fat from stock, and put that into the kettle also. Put into the frying-pan two spoonfuls of butter, and when it boils up stir in four of dry flour, stir until a dark-brown (but not burned), and when the soup boils up stir this in. Now braid half of the brains (which you tied in a muslin cloth, and boiled with the head), and stir them in. Stir in also a spoonful of walnut catsup, one of mushroom catsup, and one of tomato catsup. Boil two hours, and then put in the face cut in very small strips, one glass of port wine, and one lemon cut into thin slices, and let it boil up once, and dish. When in the tureen, put in the egg balls. To make the egg balls, boil four eggs ten minutes, drop them in cold water, and take out the yolks and pound them in the mortar until they are reduced to a paste, then beat them with one teaspoonful of salt, a little pepper, and the white of one egg. Make them into round balls the size of a walnut, roll them in flour, and fry them brown in butter, being careful not to burn them. They are now ready for the soup.

Oyster Soup.

Wash one quart of oysters, if they are solid, in one quart of cold water; if not, one pint of water; drain the water through a cullender into the soup-kettle; set the kettle on the fire, and when the liquor comes to a boil, skim it; then add one quart of rich new milk; just before it comes to a boil, turn in the oysters, and thicken with two spoonfuls of corn starch wet with milk; then stir in half a cup of butter, and season with pepper and salt. Let this boil up once, and serve immediately. Be very careful that they do not burn. A safe way is to boil the milk in a basin, which is set into another of water, and then turn it on the oysters just before removing it from the fire.

FISH.

Baked Cod and Salmon.

TAKE a fish weighing eight or nine pounds, wash and dry it; then lay in the pan, and skewer to keep the head and tail together. Stuff the belly and eyes with a stuffing made of chopped pork, pounded biscuit, sweet herbs, pepper, salt, onions, and butter. Sew up the belly, and bake two hours. Flour well and baste often. Make the gravy in the following manner: Stir into one pint of boiling water two spoonfuls of flour wet with cold water, one spoonful catsup, a pinch of ground mace, half a teaspoon of ground parsley, and a glass of red wine; salt and pepper. Let this boil, and when the fish is dished, stir the gravy that is in the pan into the made gravy. Add the wine the last thing. Garnish the fish with sliced lemon and the yolks of hard boiled eggs.

Scalloped Fish.

Skin and cut into small pieces a cod or haddock, and lay in a deep earthen dish. Dredge in about half a cup of flour, one spoonful of salt, one teaspoonful of pepper. Cut about two spoonfuls of butter into small pieces and strew in; cover the whole with new milk, and bake forty minutes.

POULTRY.

To Clean Poultry.

FIRST singe over blazing paper or alcohol; then cut off the feet and tips of the wings, and the neck as far as it looks dark; then, with the blade of a knife, take out all the pin-feathers; now turn the skin of the neck back, and with the fore-finger and thumb draw out the crop and wind-pipe; cut a slit in the lower part of the fowl, and draw out the intestines, being careful not to break the gall-bag, as it will spoil the flavor of the meat. It will be found near the upper part of the breast-bone and attached to the liver. Now wash thoroughly in several waters, and drain. If the poultry is at all strong, let it stand in water several hours, with either charcoal or saleratus. Split the gizzard, and take out the inside and inner lining; wash and put on to boil in two quarts of cold water (this is for the gravy).

Roast Turkey.

Prepare as directed; make a dressing with six pounded crackers, one teaspoonful of pepper, one tablespoonful of salt, one of sage, one of summer-savory, one of parsley, two eggs, butter the size of an egg, and cold water to moisten; stuff the turkey with this; stuff the breast first, and the remainder put in the body. Now cross and tie the legs down tight; run a skewer through the wings, fastening them to the body; fasten the neck under the body with a skewer, and tie all with a twine. Rub the turkey with salt, and spit it; baste often with the drippings and flour, and occasionally with butter. About fifteen minutes before dishing baste with butter, and dredge on a little flour; this will give it a frothy appearance. For eight pounds, allow one hour and three quarters, if roasted in the tin-kitchen; if in the oven, one hour and half, and fifteen minutes for every pound more or less. Serve with giblet gravy and cranberry sauce.

To make the gravy: Boil the heart, gizzard, liver, and neck in two quarts of water two hours; then take them up and chop the gizzard and heart; braid the liver and put them back again; thicken with one spoonful of flour wet with cold water; season with salt and pepper. Let this simmer one hour longer, and when you dish the turkey turn the drippings into this gravy; boil up once, and send to the table. Make all the gravy for poultry in this manner, omitting the chopped gizzards in chicken gravy.

Roast Chicken.

Prepare, stuff and truss the same as turkey. A pair of chickens, weighing each two and a half pounds, will require an hour and a quarter to roast if in the tin-kitchen; one hour if in the oven.

Roast Goose.

Prepare, as directed for poultry, and stuff the body with a dressing made in the following manner: Pare and boil potatoes; mash them and mix with one fourth of an onion chopped fine, one spoonful of sage, one of salt, one teaspoonful of pepper, a small piece of butter. Truss, and roast (if it weighs ten pounds) one hour and three quarters if in the tin-kitchen, but if in the oven one hour and a half. Make the gravy as for turkey, and serve with apple-sauce.

Skim off all the fat before putting the drippings in the gravy.

Roast Duck.

Prepare the dressing as for goose, and roast before a hot fire forty minutes, or if in the oven have it very hot and roast thirty minutes. Serve with either apple-sauce or currant jelly. Make gravy the same as for turkey.

This time cooks the goose and ducks rare.

Roast Partridges.

Clean and truss; then lard and roast thirty minutes. Serve with currant jelly. To make the gravy: Put one spoonful of butter into a basin, and when it boils up stir in one spoonful of dry flour; stir until a dark brown; then pour on half a pint of boiling water. Season with salt, pepper, the partridge drippings, and a spoonful of currant jelly. Or serve with bread sauce, the rule for which you will find under sauces.

To lard a bird: Cut fat salt pork into thin, narrow slices, and put one end of the slice through the eye of a larding needle. (You can obtain one at any kitchen furnishing store.) Now run the needle under the skin of the bird, and draw the pork half way through, having the pieces about an inch apart.

Roast Grouse.

If you stuff them, make the dressing the same as for turkey; but they are not often stuffed. Roast thirty minutes, and serve with currant jelly. The gravy made the same as before directed.

Roast Pigeons.

Lard and roast the same as partridges. Make the gravy the same, with the addition of one teaspoonful of clove and half a wineglass of claret. The pigeons must be young, or they will not be nice roasted.

Small Birds.

Woodcock, quail, snipe, and plover may be cooked in the same manner as partridges, allowing fifteen minutes to roast, and serve on toast.

VENISON.

Roast Venison.

If in winter keep the venison three weeks after being killed; but if in summer, ten or twelve days will be sufficient. Draw the dry skin from a leg of venison, and cut off the shank; roast half an hour, and then baste with salt, water, butter, and flour; when it has roasted one hour and a half, baste with claret wine. If it is to be served on blazers, two hours will cook a leg weighing fifteen pounds, but if not, roast four hours. A saddle of venison is cooked in the same way, but will require only half as much time to roast. To make the gravy, put the shank in a basin with three quarts of cold water, a few cloves, one onion, half a pound of beef, salt, and pepper; boil until there is about a quart of liquor, then strain, and thicken with two spoonfuls of flour. When the venison is dished add the drippings and one glass of claret wine. Boil up once and serve. Have the dishes on which the venison is served and the plates very *hot*.

Venison steak and pie is cooked the same as beef.

ENTREMETS.

Stewed Beef with Mushrooms.

VERY nice. Take five pounds of beef (with as much tenderloin as possible), put in a pan, and set in the oven fifteen minutes; then take the meat and put it in a small porcelain kettle, and dredge with salt, pepper, a teaspoonful of mace, half of clove, half of allspice, and two spoonfuls of flour; now put in cold water enough to cover the meat, and stew slowly, keeping the steam in, three hours. Then put in half a tumbler of mushroom catsup and a glass of claret wine, and simmer half an hour longer. Serve with plenty of gravy.

Fillet of Beef with Mushrooms.

Cut the fillet into slices about half an inch thick, and lay them an hour in melted butter, having first sprinkled them with salt and pepper. At the end of that time place them over a brisk fire, and when well browned on one side turn them and brown on the other. Then lay them in a hot dish, and into the butter that remains in the pan put one spoonful of dry flour, and brown; when brown, add half a cup of boiling water, and half a wineglass of mushroom catsup or maderia wine. Pour the gravy over the fillet, and serve.

Alamode Beef.

Take six pounds of the round of beef, cut deep gashes in it, and rub into it a handful of salt, a spoonful of cinnamon, half of clove, half of allspice, one of mace, one of pepper, and half a cup of flour. Fill the gashes with dressing made as for turkey, with the addition of a little chopped onion. Sew the gashes together, and bind the beef with strips of cotton cloth. Lay the beef in a small kettle that can be covered tight; put in a whole onion and cold water enough to cover the beef. Simmer three hours, and then make a thickening with four spoonfuls of flour, and stir in, and at the same time stir in two spoonfuls of either mushroom or walnut catsup and simmer one hour longer. Some persons think that the addition of a glass of claret or Madeira is an improvement; but it is very nice without.

Bouilli Beef.

Take six pounds of lean beef and rub into it two spoonfuls of salt, one half of pepper, one cup of flour; then lay in a small kettle, which you can cover tight. Cut into this one carrot, one small turnip, one onion, two parsnips, and cover with cold water. When it comes to a boil skim, then set back where it will simmer three hours; at the end of this time thicken with three spoonfuls of flour, and cut in three potatoes; cover and simmer again one hour. If not seasoned enough, add more salt and pepper.

ENTREMETS.

Bouilli Tongue.

Boil and skin the tongue the day before, and prepare in the same way as bouilli beef, allowing it two hours to simmer.

Stewed Partridges.

Place two partridges in a small kettle, and dredge with salt, pepper, flour, half a teaspoonful of mace, half of cloves, and cover with cold water. Cover tight and simmer two hours. Thicken with three spoonfuls of flour, and stir in two spoonfuls of catsup; simmer one hour longer and serve. Grouse and pigeons are stewed in the same manner. Garnish all the foregoing dishes with paste cakes.

Brown Fricassee of Chicken.

Cut two chickens or old fowl into handsome pieces, and parboil them in just water enough to cover them; when they are tender, take them up and drain them dry. Cut a pound of salt pork into slices, and fry them brown; take up the pork, dredge the chicken with salt, pepper, and flour, and fry a dark brown in the pork fat. When the chicken is all fried, stir into the remaining pork fat half a cup of dry flour; stir this until a dark brown, then pour on it one quart of the liquor in which the chicken was boiled. (This liquor must be boiling.) Season with pepper and salt to taste. Lay the chicken in this gravy, and simmer twenty minutes. Garnish the dish with boiled rice.

White Fricassee of Chicken.

Boil the chicken until tender, then cut it into small pieces. With the water in which it was boiled make a gravy, allowing half a cup of flour and two spoonfuls of butter to every quart of water. Season with pepper and salt; turn in the chicken, and let it boil five minutes, and serve. Garnish the dish with boiled rice.

Chicken Curry.

Make the same as white fricassee, with the addition of one teaspoonful of Indian curry to one pint of gravy, if it is liked strong, if not, half a teaspoonful. Dissolve the curry in a little water, and stir in. Garnish the dish with rice. Veal and mutton can be curried in the same manner.

Chicken Pie.

Prepare the chicken as for white fricassee; turn into a deep earthen dish and cover with a paste, and bake one hour.

Salad Dressing.

One tablespoonful of mustard, one of sugar, one teaspoonful of salt, one tenth of cayenne pepper, and the yolks of three uncooked eggs. Put this mixture in an earthen dish and set on ice; stir with a wooden or silver spoon until it is all well mixed, then add, very gradually, one bottle of table oil. Stir until very light;

then stir in half a cup of vinegar. One cup of whipped cream is a great addition to it; stir in the last thing. Be sure that you stir evenly, and *one way* all the time. This is enough for four quarts of salad.

Broiled Chicken.

Split down the back, wash, and wipe dry, and broil over clear coals twenty-five minutes. Season with pepper, salt and butter.

Chicken Salad.

Boil tender four good-sized chickens; when cold; cut off the white meat, and chop rather coarse. Cut off the white part of the celery and chop in the same manner. To two quarts and a pint of the chicken allow one quart and a pint of the celery and a spoonful of salt. Mix well together, and then stir in part of the dressing. Shape the salad in a flat dish, and pour over the remainder of the dressing. Garnish with hard boiled eggs, beets, and the tops of the celery.

Lobster Salad.

Lobster salad is made the same as chicken, using lobster instead of chicken, and lettuce instead of celery.

Chicken Patties.

Make the shell as for tarts, only larger, and prepare the chicken as for white fricassee, but cutting it smaller, and taking out all the bones. Fill the shells, and send to the table immediately.

Devilled Turkey.

Take the legs (the first and second joints) of a roast turkey (if underdone they are still better), and cut deep gashes in them, and into these gashes put a little mixed mustard, a little salt and cayenne pepper; lay on the gridiron until heated through; then place on a very hot dish, and spread with butter. Serve immediately. Any kind of fowl may be served in the same way.

Potted Pigeon.

Clean, then stuff the pigeons with a dressing made as for turkey. Sew them up and truss; put them in a kettle with water enough to cover them, and boil half an hour, then take up and drain them. Roll them in flour, and fry *brown* in pork fat. Thicken the liquor in which they were boiled with flour, pepper, salt, cloves, mace, and catsup. Put the pigeons in this gravy and simmer two hours. Serve in the gravy. Add half a glass of claret if you choose.

Pigeon Pie.

Prepare as for stewed pigeons, then turn into a deep earthen dish, and cover with paste. Bake forty-five minutes.

Quail Pie.

Lay the birds in a deep earthen dish, and season with pepper, salt, and a little butter; then dredge in flour. Nearly cover with cold water; cover with a paste, and bake one hour.

Snipe Pie.

Made the same as quail pie.

Oyster Pie.

Line a tin plate with plain paste, and then put in two dozen oysters, sprinkle with a little pepper, salt, and grate on a little nutmeg. Strew in a little butter, and cover with a rich paste. Bake twenty minutes, and serve immediately.

Oyster Patties.

Make the shell the same as for chicken patties. Put one quart of oysters in a basin with their own liquor, and let them boil three minutes. Season with a little salt, pepper, and a heaping spoonful of butter; fill the shells with this, and send to the table immediately.

Oyster Roast.

Cook the same as for patties, but serve on buttered toast.

Scalloped Oysters.

Put a layer of oysters in an oval dish, and dredge in a little salt, pepper, and butter; then a layer of rolled cracker, and another of oysters; dredge the oyssters as before, and cover with cracker; over the cracker grate a little nutmeg, and lay on small pieces of butter. Bake twenty minutes in a quick oven; add a glass of Maderia wine if you choose. Allow four crackers, two spoonfuls of butter, and one teaspoonful of pepper to one quart of oysters. Fill the dish to within an inch of the top.

Fried Oysters.

Drain the oysters on a sieve; roll them in cracker crumbs, and fry in *boiling* lard a light brown. Serve on brown-bread toast. When you desire them fried in batter, make one as for apple fritters, and fry in boiling lard. Have the dishes very hot.

Broiled Oysters.

Prepare in crumbs as for frying, and broil a light brown. Examine oysters carefully to see that there are not pieces of shell among them. Some oysters need more salt than others.

Veal Croquettes.

Chop *finè* two pounds of cold veal; season with one teaspoonful of pepper, one tablespoonful of salt, one of butter. Mix with this two eggs and one fourth of a cup of water. Mix this thoroughly, and make into pear shapes about the size of an egg. Have two well-beaten eggs; dip the croquettes into them, and fry a light brown in boiling lard.

Rice Croquettes.

Boil one cup of rice, as for a vegetable, and when cool, mix with four well-beaten eggs, one grated nutmeg, half a cup of sugar, and if not salt enough, a little more salt. Make into pear shapes about the size of an egg, then dip in well-beaten egg, and fry in lard a light brown.

Macaroni in Cream.

Wash a pint of macaroni, and then put in a basin with cold milk; set this into another basin with some water, and let it stand on the fire twenty minutes; then take off, and when it gets cold, stir in one teaspoonful of salt and three well-beaten eggs; turn this into a shallow dish, and bake twenty minutes.

Queen Fritters.

Into half a pint of boiling water stir half a cup of butter, and when this boils up, stir in one pint of flour; let this cook about five minutes, beating well all the time; then take off, and turn into an earthen dish. When this is cool, break five eggs into a dish, but do not beat them; turn one third of the eggs into the dish with the paste, and beat all together with the hand. When this is well mixed, turn in half of the remainder; beat as before, and then add the remainder of the egg, and beat twenty minutes. Drop this paste in teaspoonfuls into boiling lard, and fry until they crack open (this will be in about fifteen or twenty minutes). Serve with or without sugar and wine.

Plain Fritters.

Beat to a froth two eggs, and stir into this half a pint of milk, one teaspoonful of salt, two cups of flour; beat this lightly, and drop by teaspoonfuls into boiling lard, and fry a light brown.

Apple Fritters.

Make the batter as for plain fritters. Pare and core nice tart apples; cut them in thin slices, dip them in the batter, and fry brown.

Pancakes.

Beat to a froth three eggs; stir into this half a pint of milk, one teaspoonful of salt, and three tablespoonfuls of flour. Heat the frying-pan, and grease well with butter; turn one third of the batter into it, and fry a light brown on one side, shaking the pan frequently to prevent burning. When brown on one side, turn and brown the other. When done, spread with jelly, fold, and serve immediately. You can omit the jelly, and spread with sugar, if you choose.

PUDDINGS.

Baltimore Pudding.

ONE cup of molasses, one of milk, one of chopped suet, one of chopped raisins, three and a half of flour, one teaspoonful of saleratus, one tablespoonful of cinnamon, one teaspoonful of cloves, one of mace, one of allspice, and one grated nutmeg. Beat the molasses, suet, raisins, and spice together; then stir in the milk, in which dissolve the saleratus, then the flour. Steam five hours or more. You cannot steam it too much. This pudding is nicer the second day than the first. Serve with wine sauce.

Wedding Pudding.

One cup of clear salt pork chopped fine, one of chopped raisins, two of sugar, three and a half of flour, one of milk, one teaspoonful of saleratus, one of cloves, one of cinnamon. Beat together the pork, sugar, raisins, and spice, then add the milk, in which dissolve the saleratus, and then the flour. Steam four hours or more. Serve with rich wine sauce.

Plum Pudding.

One quart of bread (bakers' is the best), one quart of milk, six eggs, one cup of brown sugar, one of molasses, one of suet, one teaspoonful each of cinnamon, clove, allspice, mace, and nutmeg, one cup of currants, one of raisins, one quarter of a pound of citron. Boil the milk, and pour on the bread; let this stand one hour; then stir into it the sugar, spice, suet, raisins, and currants; beat the eggs to a froth, and stir in. Have ready a deep earthen pot well buttered, and turn the mixture into it, and bake four hours, or steam five. Serve with rich wine sauce.

Christmas Pudding.

Ten crackers, one quart of milk, five eggs, one pint of sugar, one and a half cups of chopped suet, one cup of molasses, one cup of brandy, one spoonful of salt, one nutmeg, one tablespoonful of cinnamon, two teaspoonfuls of cloves, two of allspice, two of mace, two of currants, two of raisins, and a quarter of a pound of citron. Break the crackers up and soak in the milk overnight. (Set in a cool place where it will not sour.) In the morning mix with it the sugar, molasses, suet, salt, spice, brandy, and fruit. Boil or steam five hours. Serve with a rich wine sauce.

Bread and Butter Pudding.

Butter a deep pudding-dish; cut a small brick loaf into thin slices, and butter them; lay a layer of them in the dish, and then sprinkle with raisins, currants, and thin slices of citron, then another layer of bread, and so on, until the bread is all used; cover with a custard made with nine eggs, one cup of sugar, three pints of milk, two teaspoonfuls of salt, and one nutmeg. Let this stand three hours, and then bake one hour and a half in a moderate oven. Serve with a rich wine sauce.

Snow Pudding.

Soak half a box of Cox's sparkling gelatine in half a cup of cold water two hours; pour on this nearly a pint of *boiling* water, stir until the gelatine is all dissolved, and then stir in two cups of sugar and the juice of two large lemons; stir this a few minutes, and then add the whites of six eggs. Now set the basin into another of ice-water, being careful not to let it come over the basin in which the mixture is. Beat this until it is white and stiff; turn into the dish in which it is to be served, and set on the ice until the last moment.

Sauce for Snow Pudding.

Beat together the yolks of six eggs and half a cup of sugar; add to this two spoonfuls milk and half a teaspoonful of salt. Put one pint of milk into a small pail; set the pail into a basin of boiling water (be careful that it does boil into the milk); let this come to a boil, and then stir in the eggs. Stir this two minutes, and then take off and set in ice-water; stir occasionally until cool. Have it ice cold and flavor with vanilla.

Cocoanut Pudding.

One quart of milk, one teaspoonful of butter, the yolks and the whites of three eggs, one cup of sugar, one cocoanut and milk of cocoanut. Bore a hole in the cocoanut and drain out the milk; then crack the nut and take from the shell; pare off the brown skin and grate. Butter a pudding-dish and lay the cocoanut in it, then pour over it the custard. (Scald the milk before making the custard.) Bake in a moderate oven until it is firm in the centre, which you can tell by cutting with the handle of a teaspoon. Frost immediately upon taking from the oven, with the whites of two eggs and one cup of sugar beaten to a stiff froth.

Cocoanut Pudding, No. 2.

Six eggs, one cup of sugar, one quart of milk, one cocoanut, milk of cocoanut. Prepare the cocoanut as for No. 1. Beat the eggs and sugar to a froth, stir in the milk and then the cocoanut; butter a pudding-dish, turn in the mixture, and bake twenty or thirty minutes. When the fresh cocoanut is not in the market, use one cup of the desiccated cocoanut and the juice of one fresh lemon.

Ginger Pudding.

One cup of butter, two of sugar, one of milk, four of flour, one tablespoonful of ginger, one teaspoonful of saleratus, two of cream of tartar, four eggs. Beat the sugar and butter to a cream, then stir in the eggs, which are well beaten; then the milk, and last the flour, in which the saleratus, ginger, and cream of tartar are well mixed. Bake in a pudding-dish forty-five minutes. Serve with lemon or vinegar sauce.

Beverly Pudding.

Pare, boil, and mash six good-sized potatoes; pour over them one quart of *boiling* milk; stir well, and let it get cold; then add to it the yolks of five eggs, and the whites of three, beaten with one large cup of sugar, the grated rind and juice of two lemons. Bake thirty minutes, and then frost with the whites of two eggs and one cup of sugar beaten to a stiff froth; set back in the oven until it is a delicate brown, then set away to cool. To be eaten ice cold.

Lemon Pudding.

One quart of milk, a piece of butter the size of an egg, one heaping cup of sugar, one cup of ground rice, the rind and juice of two lemons, six eggs. Take one cup of milk from the quart, and put the remainder in a tin pail; set the pail into a basin of boiling water Wet the rice with the cup of cold milk, and when the milk begins to boil, stir it into it with one teaspoonful of salt; let this boil ten minutes, then take off and let it get blood warm. Beat the eggs, sugar, and lemon together, and stir into the mixture. Bake in a buttered dish half an hour. To be eaten cold.

Lemon Pudding, No. 2.

One cup of flour, butter the size of a small egg, three pints of milk, eight eggs, the grated rind of four and the juice of two lemons. Rub the butter and flour together, add the beaten eggs, and stir all into the boiling milk; set this away to cool, and when cold, add the lemon and three cups of sugar. Line the pudding-dish with paste, or not, as you choose. Bake thirty five or forty minutes.

Corn Pudding.

Put one quart of popped corn into a pudding-dish; stir into one quart of milk two teaspoonfuls of salt, and turn the milk on the corn. Bake twenty minutes. Serve with sugar and cream.

Boiled Cherry Pudding.

One brick loaf soaked until soft in one pint of new milk; then add three eggs well beaten, and one quart of ripe cherries. Boil two hours and a half. Serve with either wine or vinegar sauce.

Baked Whortleberry Pudding.

One cup of butter, two of sugar, four of flour, one of sour milk, five eggs, one teaspoonful of saleratus, four cups of berries. Beat the sugar and butter to a cream; then add the eggs, which have been well beaten, then the milk, in which the saleratus is dissolved, and lastly, the berries. Bake one hour, and serve with a rich wine sauce.

Appledore Pudding.

Butter a pudding-dish and line it with stale cake; then fill it within three inches of the top with blueberries, blackberries, or currants. To one quart of blueberries or blackberries allow half a cup of sugar, if currants allow one cupful. Cover the whole with cake, and wet with half a tumbler of wine. Bake half an hour, and frost with the whites of two eggs and one cup of sugar beaten to a stiff froth; set back in the oven, and bake a light brown. To be eaten without sauce.

Bird's Nest Pudding.

Pare and core six large apples (being careful not to break them). Make a syrup of one quart of water and one cup of sugar; simmer the apples in this until they are tender, but not so tender but that they will keep their shape; lay them in a pudding-dish, and cover with a custard made with one quart of milk, five eggs, and three spoonfuls of sugar. Bake until the custard is firm. May be eaten either cold or hot, and without sauce.

Rice Meringue.

Two cups of boiled rice, one quart of milk, the yolks of six eggs and the whites of four, two spoonfuls of sugar one teaspoonful of salt, half a teaspoonful of the extract of lemon. Bake thirty-five minutes; then frost with the whites of two eggs, one and a half cups of sugar, one tablespoonful of corn starch, beaten to a stiff froth. Flavor with lemon. Bake a light brown, and serve hot without sauce.

Pavilion Pudding.

Lay in a mould alternate layers of fruit and silver cake. (Cut the slices about two inches thick.) Make a custard with six eggs, one quart of milk, and one teaspoonful of salt. Pour this over the cake, and let it stand in a cool place two hours; then steam three hours. Serve with a rich sauce.

Frozen Pudding.

Place in a mould slices of light cake, and between them any kind of preserves; when the mould is nearly full, cover with cold soft custard. (Dissolve a spoonful of gelatine in the custard when you make it.) Cover the mould and pack in a box of salt and ice, as you would ice cream. Let this stand in the salt and ice five hours. When you dish it dip the mould in a pail of hot water for one instant, wipe the mould, take off the cover, and turn the pudding out. Serve immediately. Be sure that the cover of the mould is so tight that it will not admit one drop of water. It should be made of block tin.

Fruit Pudding.

Take one quart of cake crumbs and mix with a custard made of a pint and a half of milk, four eggs, one spoonful of sugar, two spoonfuls of wine, and a little nutmeg; let this stand half an hour, and then stir in half a cup of currants, one cup of raisins, and a few strips of citron. Butter a pudding-dish and turn in this mixture. Bake one hour. Serve with a rich wine sauce.

Almond Pudding.

Pound to a paste one pint of blanched almonds. Boil one quart of milk, and into it, while boiling, stir in the almonds and two spoonfuls of flour, mixed with cold milk, one teaspoonful of salt; cook this ten minutes. Let this get cool, and add five well-beaten eggs and half a teaspoonful of bitter almond, with one cup of sugar. Bake thirty minutes. Serve cold or hot.

Sunderland Pudding.

Beat to a froth six eggs. Mix gradually one quart of milk with one cup of flour; stir into this the eggs and one teaspoonful of salt. Bake twenty minutes in little earthen cups, such as you bake drop cakes in. Serve immediately with rich sauce.

Pine Apple Pudding.

Butter a pudding dish, and line the sides with slices of stale sponge cake. Pare and cut a large pineapple into thin slices; place a layer of it in the bottom of the dish, and sprinkle with sugar, then another layer, and so on, until the dish is nearly full; then pour over the whole two thirds of a cup of cold water, and cover the whole with slices of cake which have been dipped in cold water. Cover the whole with a plate, and bake slowly two hours. Serve with sugar and cream. (Use in all one cup of sugar.) Bread may be used instead of cake.

Omelet Souffle.

Beat together the yolks of four eggs and two spoonfuls of sugar; then beat to a froth the whites of eight eggs and stir into the yolks and sugar. Flavor with half a teaspoonful of bitter almond. Turn into a buttered dish and bake twelve minutes. Serve instantly.

PIES.

Puff Paste.

Two cups of butter, one quart of flour, one tablespoonful of salt, one of powdered sugar. Wash the butter in cold water until it is light and waxy; divide into two parts and set in the ice chest one hour. Mix the sugar and salt with the dry flour, and then wet with ice-water enough to make a soft paste (mix with a knife, and use the hands as little as possible); roll this on the board with the rolling-pin, about half an inch thick; now cut one of the cakes of washed butter into thin slices, and spread on the paste; dredge with flour and *fold* up; then pound lightly with the pin, and then roll out as before, and spread the second cake of butter the same as the first; dredge and *fold* again; now roll thin as before, and then *roll* up and place on a plate, and set in the ice chest one or two hours. When ready to cover the pie, cut just enough from the end of the roll to cover the pie; sprinkle the board with a little flour, place the paste upon it, and flour the rolling-pin with the hand; now roll *from* you, and towards your left hand; roll very lightly until the right size; then cover and bake immediately. *Quickness* and *elasticity* are very important, also the washing of the butter. Use as little flour as possible in rolling the paste; always make it in a cool room. It is a mistake to think the paste must be hard to be good; always have it soft enough to roll easily.

Green Apple Pies.

Pare, quarter, core, and stew nice tart apples in water enough to prevent them from burning. When tender, sweeten very sweet with white sugar, fill the pie-plate, which has been lined and edged with paste, grate on a little nutmeg, cover and bake forty-five minutes.

Dried Apple Pies.

Pick and wash one quart of dried apples, and put in a porcelain kettle with two quarts of water and two of cider; let this stand over night, and in the morning place on the fire and simmer three hours; then lay in (but do not stir) two quarts of sugar, and simmer two hours longer; then turn into a stone pot, and put away for use. Make the pies the same as green apple.

Peach Pies.

Line the plate with plain paste, and lay in the plate five peaches, which just press between the fingers, but do not take out the stones, as they flavor the pie; now fill the plate with peaches which have been cut in two and the stones taken out. Sift over this a small cup of sugar, and then add two spoonfuls of water. Cover and bake in a moderate oven one hour. Do not peel the peaches; they are very much better not to be.

Plum Pies.

Made the same as peach.

Mince Pies.

Two pounds of tender lean beef; chop it while raw very fine; take one cupful of chopped suet, two pint bowlfuls of chopped apple, one of stoned raisins, half a bowlful of currants, half a pound of citron, one bowlful of sugar, one half of molasses, two tablespoonfuls of mace, two of cinnamon, one of allspice, one of cloves, four grated nutmegs, three tablespoonfuls of salt. Mix all this thoroughly with the hands, and then add one quart of cider. Put the mixture in a large earthen pan, and place over a kettle of boiling water and scald; if there is not sugar and spice enough, season to taste. When scalded, stir in one pint of wine and half a pint of brandy. Do not let any one kind of spice predominate. If not moist enough, use more cider. Prepare the plates as for apple pies, and spread in a cupful of the mince meat and cover with a rich puff paste. Bake one hour.

Lemon Pies.

Line a medium-sized plate with plain paste, and rim with three thicknesses of puff paste; set the plate in a cool place until the filling is ready. Beat to a froth one teacup of sugar, the rind and juice of one lemon, and the yolks of two eggs; then beat the whites of two eggs to a stiff froth, and stir in with one spoonful of milk; turn this into the plate which you have prepared, and bake in a moderate oven forty-five minutes. Or you may line a deep plate with plain paste, as for squash pies, and turn the mixture into it, and bake forty minutes. This is very nice if the directions are exactly followed.

Lemon Pies, No. 2

The juice of two and the rind of three lemons, one cup of butter, one and a half of sugar, eight eggs. Beat the sugar, butter, lemons, and the yolks of the eggs together; then add the whites beaten to a stiff froth. Bake in deep plates, line with plain paste, fifty minutes in a moderate oven.

Marlborough Pies.

Steam until tender six good-sized tart apples, and then run them through the cullender; stir in, while they are hot, one spoonful of butter; when cool, stir in the yolks of three eggs, the rind and juice of one lemon, and one teacup of sugar, which have been beaten together. Bake in a moderate oven forty minutes, in a deep plate, as squash pies. Cut and bake little cakes of puff paste, and when the pie is cold, garnish it with them.

PUDDING SAUCES.

Rich Wine Sauce.

BEAT to a cream half a cup of butter, and very gradually beat in one cup of sugar, one spoonful of corn starch, one wineglass of wine, and the white of one egg. When this is a perfect froth, stir in one third of a cup of *boiling* water; set this in warm water for two minutes, stirring all the while, and then serve.

Plain Wine Sauce.

Put into a sauce-pan one cup of sugar and one cup of water; grate into this half a nutmeg, and put on the fire to simmer; let it simmer half an hour, and then add one glass of wine; simmer ten minutes longer, and serve.

Lemon Sauce.

Beat to a froth one spoonful of butter, one cup of sugar, one spoonful of corn starch, and two eggs. When very smooth and light, add one cup of *boiling* water. Set the basin into boiling water, and stir five minutes. Season with lemon, and serve.

Vinegar Sauce.

One cup of boiling water, one of sugar, one tablespoonful of flour, one of vinegar, and a little nutmeg. Mix the flour with a little cold water, and stir into the boiling sugar and water; then stir in the vinegar and nutmeg, and boil twenty minutes. Wine sauce is very good made in this manner, using wine instead of vinegar. Season with a little salt.

DISHES FOR THE SICK.

Beef Tea.

CUT half a pound of lean beef into very small pieces; do not have a grain of fat on it, and put into a bottle that has a large opening (an olive or horseradish bottle will be nice); put in half a cup of cold water, and cork tight; set this in a basin of cold water, and place on the fire where it will come to a boiling point, but not boil; keep it at this temperature for two hours, then strain, and season with salt.

Chicken Broth.

Put the bones and about one pound of the lean meat of chicken into a sauce-pan with three pints of water. When it comes to a boil, skim well. Simmer three hours, and strain and salt. If the patient can bear it, a little rice or tapioca boiled with it is an improvement.

Oatmeal Gruel.

Into one quart of boiling water, sprinkle two tablespoonfuls of oatmeal; let this boil forty minutes; season with salt, strain and serve. If sugar, milk, or cream is wished, it may be added.

Indian Meal Gruel.

One quart of boiling water; stir into this one spoonful of flour and two of Indian meal, mixed with a little cold water. Boil thirty minutes. Season with salt, and strain. Use sugar and cream if you choose. If flour is not liked, use another spoonful of meal instead.

Plum Porridge.

Into one quart of boiling milk stir two spoonfuls of flour mixed with cold milk; put in a handful of raisins and a little grated nutmeg. Boil twenty minutes. Season with salt and strain.

Corn Tea.

Brown and pound in a mortar, one cup of sweet dry corn; pour on this two cups of boiling water, and steep fifteen minutes. This is very light and nutritious, and can be taken where the patient is very weak.

Cream Toast.

Heat half a cup of cream, and season with salt. Toast two slices of bread a light brown, and pour the cream over it. Serve immediately.

Wine Whey.

Let one cup of new milk come to a boil, and then stir in half a wineglass of sherry wine. Boil a moment and strain.

Vinegar Whey.

Boil one cup of milk, and stir in one spoonful of vinegar; if this does not make it whey, stir in a little more; when it curdles, strain.

Sour Milk Whey.

To one cup of boiling sweet milk, and one cup of sour milk, and strain.

A Good Drink for the Lungs.

Wash clean a few pieces of Irish moss; put it in a pitcher, and pour over it two cups of boiling water. Set where it will keep at the boiling point, but not boil for two hours. Strain, and squeeze into it the juice of one lemon. Sweeten to taste. If the patient cannot take lemon, flavor with wine, vanilla, or nutmeg.

Another Drink.

Beat lightly one egg and one spoonful of sugar. Stir into this one cup of new milk, half a wineglass of wine, and a little nutmeg. This is nice without the wine.

Another Drink.

Upon one teaspoonful of slippery-elm, pour one cup of boiling water, strain, and season as Irish moss.

Lemonade.

The juice of one lemon and one spoonful of sugar. Pour on this one cup of boiling water, and set away to cool.

Another Beef Tea.

Cut a pound of lean beef (the round is the best) into dice. Put into a sauce-pan, with a teaspoonful of salt, one of flour, and one fourth of pepper. Pour on this a large pint of cold water. Let it stand an hour or two, then put on the fire; bring slowly to a boil, and boil slowly an hour. If it has boiled away too much, add a little hot water; but this rather hurts it. Skim off carefully every particle of fat. This tea is more palatable than the other, and can be taken by those not extremely sick.

Sack Posset.

Pound one Boston cracker, or one soda biscuit. Put it in a pint of cold milk; set on the fire, and simmer fifteen minutes. Beat together one egg, one wineglass of wine, a little sugar, salt, and nutmeg. Turn this into the simmering milk, stirring constantly; boil up once, and take from the fire immediately.

DESSERTS.

Charlotte Russe.

Cut stale sponge cake into slices about half an inch thick, and line three moulds with it, having a space of half an inch between each slice; set the moulds where they will not be disturbed until the filling is ready. Now take a deep tin pan and fill about one third full of either snow or pounded ice, and into this set another pan that will hold at least four quarts. Into a deep bowl or pail, put one pint and a half of cream (if the cream is *thick* take one pint of cream and half a pint of *milk*), whip the cream to a froth, and when the bowl is full, skim the froth into the pan which is setting on the ice; keep on doing this until the cream is all froth; now with the spoon draw the froth to one side, and you shall find that there is some of the cream which has gone back to milk; turn this into the bowl again, and whip as before; when the cream is all whipped, stir into it two thirds of a cup of powdered sugar, one teaspoonful of vanilla, and half a box of gelatine, which has been soaked in cold water, enough to cover it, one hour, and then dissolved in boiling water enough to dissolve it, which will be nearly half a cupful; stir all this from the bottom of the pan until it begins to grow stiff; then fill the moulds, and set them on the ice in the pan for one hour, or until they are sent to the table.

When ready to dish them, just loosen them at the sides, and turn out on a flat dish. Have the cream ice cold when you begin to whip it; it is a good plan to put a lump of ice into the cream while you are whipping it.

The directions being so long, may make it appear to be a long and hard process; but it is not so, for it is easily and quickly made. The whip-churn you can get made at your tinman's for a trifle, and as it will be found necessary to have one to make many of these dishes, I give below directions for making it.

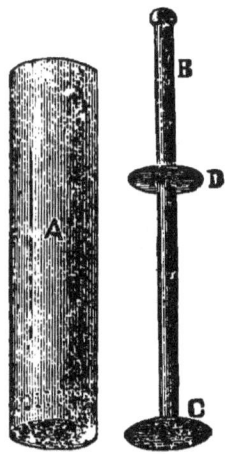

A, is a hollow cylinder of tin, perforated in the bottom and upon the sides, as represented above.
B, handle.
C, dash of tin, and perforated like the bottom of the cylinder.
D, cover, fitting close upon the upper end of the cylinder. Have the cylinder three inches in diameter, and ten inches in height: the dash two and three-quarters inches in diameter, and the handle thirteen inches long. To be made of block tin. With care this will last in a private family fifty years.

NOTE.—The whip-churn, for making Charlotte Russe and creams, can be procured at Sweetser and Clark's, Market Street, Portsmouth, N. H., and at F. A. Walker & Co.'s, 83 and 85 Cornhill, and Nos. 6 & 8 Brattle Street, Boston, Mass.

Holland Cream.

Make the same as Charlotte Russe, omitting the cake and vanilla. Flavor with half a wineglass of Holland gin. Shape in blanc-mange moulds.

DESSERTS.

Lemon Cream.

The grated rind of one and the juice of two lemons, a pint of water, one pint of sugar, six eggs. Beat the whites of the eggs and the lemon together, then add the water; let this stand one hour; then stir in the pint of sugar and the yolks of the six eggs, and place over a gentle fire, until it thickens. *Stir continually.* When it is thick, set one side until it is cool enough to turn into glasses; then fill the glasses, and set where they will get very cold.

Velvet Cream.

Make the same as Charlotte Russe, omitting the cake and vanilla, and flavoring with half a wineglass of wine. Shape in blanc-mange moulds.

Italian Cream.

Make the same as Charlotte Russe, omitting the cake, and adding five well-beaten eggs. Shape in blanc-mange moulds.

Chocolate Cream.

Soak one box of gelatine in cold water enough to cover it one hour. Put one quart of rich milk into a tin pail, and set in a kettle with hot water to boil. Scrape two ounces of French chocolate, and mix with eight spoonfuls of sugar; wet this with two spoonfuls of the boiling milk, and rub with the bowl of the spoon until a smooth paste, then stir into the boiling milk; now stir in the gelatine, and then stir in the yolks of ten well beaten eggs; stir three minutes, take off and strain; set in a pan of ice water; stir for ten minutes, then add two spoonfuls of vanilla, and put into blanc-mange moulds; set away on the ice for three hours. Serve with sugar and cream.

Blanc-mange made with Gelatine.

Soak a box of gelatine in cold water enough to cover it one hour. Put three pints of milk in a tin pail, and set in a kettle with hot water; when the milk comes to a boil, stir in the gelatine and two spoonfuls of sugar. Flavor with vanilla or lemon, strain into blanc-mange moulds, and when cool, set on ice to harden. Make this, if possible, the day before it is to be used. Serve with sugar and cream.

Moss Blanc-mange.

Free from pebbles and seaweed, and wash in several waters one cup of Irish moss (get that that is not pressed); let it soak in cold water one hour, then tie up in a muslin bag, and put in a tin pail with three quarts of new milk. Set the pail in a kettle with hot water, and boil thirty minutes; after it comes to a boil, stirring occasionally. Press the bag between the side of the pail and the spoon, to get out all the gluten; stir in a teaspoonful of salt, half a cup of sugar, and flavor with anything you please. Turn into blanc-mange moulds, and set away to cool. Serve with sugar and cream. This is the best kind of blanc-mange.

Blanc-mange in Wine Sauce.

Put one quart of new milk into a basin, and set the basin in another with hot water. When the milk comes to a boil, stir in four spoonfuls of corn starch mixed with half a cup of milk and one teaspoon of salt; stir and boil for ten minutes, and then turn into a blanc-mange mould. Set away to cool. When time to serve, turn into a deep dessert-dish, and pour over it the following sauce: Beat to a cream the yolks of two eggs, one heaping cup of sugar, and a wineglass of wine; then stir in the whites of two eggs, beaten to a stiff froth. Serve immediately. Always dip the moulds in cold water before filling them with blanc-mange or cream.

Wine Jelly.

Soak one box of gelatine in half a pint of cold water two hours; then pour on a pint and a half of boiling water, and stir until the gelatine is all dissolved, but do not set near the fire; now add the juice of two lemons, and sweeten to your taste. Wring a piece of thin muslin out of hot water, and lay in a fine strainer; strain the jelly through this (after adding one pint of wine to it). Make the day before using.

Lemon Jelly.

Make the same as wine jelly, using the juice of eight lemons, and one pint more water instead of the wine. This is very handsome when you make half of each kind, and cut it up in small squares, and fill wineglasses with it. Put half of each kind on a plate. Wine jelly may be colored a bright pink by using cochineal; yellow, by using tincture of saffron, and green, by using the juice of spinage; but I would not recommend the use of any coloring

Soft Custard.

Put one quart of new milk into a tin pail, and set the pail into a kettle with boiling water, and sweeten with one cup of sugar. Beat well the yolks of ten, and the whites of four eggs, and mix with them half a cup of cold milk. When the milk comes to a boil, strain the eggs into it and stir two minutes; then take off and turn into a pitcher; set the pitcher in ice water, and stir until cool. Flavor with vanilla. Serve in glasses.

Almond Custard.

Almond custard made in the same way, using the yolks of fourteen eggs and no whites, and flavor with one teaspoonful of bitter almond.

Snowball Custard.

Snowball custards are made the same as soft. Beat the whites of six eggs to a stiff froth, and drop into clear boiling water; boil two minutes, and skim out; let it drain, and when the custard is put in glasses heap this on top. They make the dish look very handsome.

Chocolate Custard.

Set one quart of milk on to boil as before directed. Scrape with a knife one ounce of nice chocolate, and mix with one heaping cup of sugar; wet this with two spoonfuls of boiling milk; work this into a paste with the back of the spoon, and stir into the boiling milk, and then stir in six well-beaten eggs; stir three minutes, and then strain. Set in cold water and stir occasionally, until cold, then stir in two teaspoons of vanilla. Serve in glasses.

Coffee Custard.

Tie one cup of ground coffee in a piece of muslin, and put on to boil with one quart of milk; let it boil ten minutes after the milk comes to a boil; then take out and stir in one heaping cup of sugar, and the whites of four and the yolks of eight eggs; stir two minutes and strain; set in cold water, and stir occasionally until cool. Serve in glass. All custards are improved by a *very little* salt.

Steamed Custards.

Make the same as for baked, and steam until they are firm in the centre.

Baked Custards.

One quart of milk, five eggs, two thirds of a cup of sugar, one teaspoonful of salt. Fill the cups, and grate over them a little nutmeg; then place in a deep pan, with warm water. Bake in a moderate oven until they are firm in the centre.

Floating Island.

Make the same as snowball custard, and serve in a deep glass dish, with the whites of the eggs heaped in the centre.

Apple Snow.

Pare, slice, and quarter ten good-sized tart apples; steam them until tender, and then run them through the cullender, and set where they will get ice cold. When cold, add the grated rind and the juice of two lemons, one cup of sugar, and the whites of six eggs. Beat all to a froth, and serve immediately in a deep glass dish.

Tipsy Parson.

Stick a large square of sponge cake full of blanched almonds, and then lay it in a deep glass dish; pour over it a tumbler of sherry, and when the wine has all soaked into the cake, fill the dish half full of soft custard.

Apple Float.

Fill a deep glass dish half full of soft custard, and then heap up with apple snow. (Make the custard with the yolks of the eggs.)

Trifle

Cut stale cake into slices, and spread preserves between them; lay in a deep glass dish, and heap the dish full of whipped cream.

Wine Whips.

Into a pint of cream, stir half a cup of sugar, half a glass of wine, and a lump of ice; whip to a froth, and fill the glasses.

Fruit Whips.

Fill the glasses one third full of any kind of preserved berries or jelly, and then fill up with whipped cream.

Mock Sherbet.

Fill a six quart pan with new-fallen snow; grate the rind and squeeze the juice of six lemons into it, and then stir in four cups of sugar. Serve immediately. This can also be made with currant jelly.

Cream Cakes.

One pint of boiling water, one cup of butter, one quart of flour, and the yolks of eight and the whites of ten eggs. Put the water and butter in a flat sauce-pan, and when it boils up, stir in all the flour at once; keep over the fire, and beat well for five minutes; then when cold break the eggs into a bowl, but do not beat; turn about three at a time on the paste, and beat all together half an hour. When light, drop on tin sheets. Have half a spoonful in a cake, and drop about two inches apart. Bake forty minutes in a rather quick oven. When baked, cut open at the sides with a small sharp pointed knife, and fill with a cream made as for cream pies. These are very nice glazed with chocolate and filled with raspberry or strawberry preserves.

Sponge Drops.

Beat to a froth three eggs and one teacup of sugar; stir into this one heaping coffee cup of flour, in which one teaspoonful of cream of tartar and half of saleratus are thoroughly mixed. Flavor with lemon. Butter tin sheets with washed butter (lard or salt butter will make them taste bad), and drop in teaspoonfuls about three inches apart. Bake instantly in a very quick oven. Watch very closely, as they will burn easily. Serve with ice cream.

Kisses.

Beat to a stiff froth the whites of two eggs, and beat into them, very gradually, two teacups of powdered sugar and two tablespoonfuls of corn starch. Flavor with lemon. Butter tin sheets with washed butter, and then cover with letter paper; drop on this the mixture in teaspoonfuls, and about two inches apart. Bake fifteen minutes in a warm oven, but be sure that it is not warm enough to brown them. After they are taken out let them stand until cold before removing them from the paper.

Cocoanut Drops.

Beat to a froth the whites of two eggs, and add gradually one small cup of sugar, and one cup of prepared cocoanut, and one spoonful of flour. Prepare the tin sheets as for kisses, and bake five minutes in a quick oven.

Cheese Cakes.

Roll puff paste about a quarter of an inch thick, and cut into two equal parts; on one part grate cheese about half an inch thick; sprinkle with water, and lay the other part over it; roll the pin lightly over this and cut into strips about two inches wide and four long; lay on tin sheets, and bake in a quick oven fifteen or twenty minutes.

Tarts.

Roll puff paste about an inch and a half thick; cut with a large cutter, and then with a smaller cutter; cut out the centre, leaving the rim about an inch wide. When you have cut out all you want, take the pieces which you cut from the centre, and roll about one quarter of an inch thick; cut this out with a large cutter, and wet with cold water; lay the rims on these, and bake in a quick oven about twenty five minutes When cold, fill with any kind of jam or jelly.

Directions for Freezing.

Set the freezer in the centre of the tub; be sure that everything is in place, or it will not work when you get it packed. Have the ice chopped fine, and put in a layer about three inches deep, then a layer of coarse salt about an inch deep, and then the ice, and so on, until the tub is full, having the ice last. Use about one third salt, and two thirds ice. It must be packed very solid. After the cream has been put in, and you have turned it ten minutes, pack again, and be sure to get it solid. When the water is troublesome, let off some, but not all. Stop the hole immediately, and pack to fill the space that was occupied by the water, as the mixture will not freeze until all air is excluded. Beat one way until you can no longer turn the beater. Now carefully brush the ice and salt from the cover and take out the beater; cover again and put a cork in the cover. Now pack again with ice and salt. Cover the whole with a piece of old carpet, and let it stand a few hours. Or if you wish to put it in moulds, fill them as soon as you take out the beater; pack them down well, or they will not look smooth when taken out. If you use an old-fashioned freezer, you must have a long iron spoon to beat it with, and a long knife to cut it from the sides with. Turn the freezer with the hands; take off the cover every fifteen minutes. Scrape the cream from the sides, and then beat, as you would cake, for ten minutes.

When hard, light, and smooth, cover as before directed, or put in moulds Lay the moulds in ice and salt for three hours, and when ready to dish, dip them in warm water for an instant. Wipe and turn the mould on an ice cream dish; remove very gently. Serve immediately

Ice Cream made with Cream.

Take four quarts of cream and sweeten with one heaping quart of sugar. Flavor with anything you please, but very strong.

Coffee Ice Cream.

Made the same as chocolate, but using coffee instead of chocolate. Tie one pint of ground coffee in a piece of muslin, and boil in the milk half an hour before; then take it out, and make as before directed.

Lemon Ice Cream.

Put two quarts of rich milk into a tin pail, and set into a kettle with hot water; when this comes to a boil, stir in four spoonfuls of corn starch; wet with one cup of milk. Cook this twenty minutes, and then add the yolks of twelve eggs, well beaten, stir a few minutes, and then take of and cool; before cooling, stir in one heaping quart of sugar. When ice cold, add two quarts of cream, or rich milk will answer, and freeze.

Vanilla, pineapple, and all other kinds of cream may be made in the same way, but use eight whites and yolks instead of twelve yolks of eggs For strawberry and raspberry cream, allow the juice of one quart of berries to one gallon of cream. Some persons object to corn starch, but it makes a very much smoother and handsomer cream than when it is all made of eggs. Where all eggs are used, make the same as soft custard, and allow one quart of cream or milk to one quart of custard.

Chocolate Ice Cream.

Made the same as the others, with the addition of one cake of chocolate, and one pint more of sugar Prepare the chocolate as for chocolate custard.

Lemon Sherbet.

One gallon of ice water, the juice of twenty lemons, and three pints of sugar; strain into the freezer, and freeze as you would cream.

Currant, strawberry, raspberry, and orange sherbets may be made in the same manner.

N. B. To flavor ice creams, use the extract. Lubin's is the best.

Roman Punch.

Two quarts of cold water, one of Madeira wine, half a pint of brandy, the juice of six lemons, and two quarts of sugar. This is very hard to freeze. In winter use snow instead of ice.

CAKE.

Remarks.

WHILE making pies and cakes, the first thing to be done is to build your fire and get your oven just right. Now sift your flour, and measure it; count and break your eggs; measure every thing you are going to put in the cake; lard your pans and line them with paper. Here is a formula, which it will be well to follow in making all kinds of cake in which you put butter.

Beat the butter to a cream, and *then* add the sugar gradually; then spice and any kind of liquor which you use, then the milk, then the eggs well beaten, then the flour, in which always mix thoroughly, while dry, the saleratus and cream of tartar, and if fruit, let that always be the last thing to be added.

One, Two, Three, Four Cake.

One coffee-cup of butter, two of sugar, four of flour, one of milk, five eggs, one teaspoonful of saleratus, two of cream of tartar, lemon. This will make two good-sized sheets. Bake one half plain, and the other half spice with one teaspoonful of cinnamon, one half of clove, the same of allspice and nutmeg. Bake in a rather quick oven.

Rich Cup Cake.

One cup of butter, two of sugar, four and a half of flour, one wine-glass of brandy, five eggs, three spoonfuls of milk, and one nutmeg. Make two loaves of this, and bake in a moderate oven fifty minutes.

Concord Cake.

One cup of butter, three of sugar, one of sour milk, four and a half of flour, five eggs, one teaspoonful of saleratus, and the rind and juice of one lemon. Make into two loaves, and bake in a moderate oven fifty minutes.

Lemon Cake.

One teacup of butter, three of sugar, four and a half of flour, one of sweet milk, five eggs, the yolks and whites beaten separately, one teaspoonful of cream of tartar, half of saleratus, and the rind and juice of one lemon. Bake in two loaves, in a rather quick oven, forty-five minutes.

Harrison Cake.

One and a half cups of butter, one and a half of sugar, one and a half of molasses, one and a half of milk, six of flour, three eggs, one glass of brandy, one teaspoonful of saleratus, one tablespoonful of cloves, one of allspice, two of cinnamon, two of mace, one pound of raisins, one of currants, quarter of a pound of citron, lemon. Bake in

CAKE. 177

three loaves, two hours and a half, in a moderate oven. This will keep twelve months.

Bangor Cake.

Two thirds of a cup of butter, two of sugar, one half of milk, three of flour, three eggs, one teaspoonful of cream of tartar, one half of saleratus. Flavor to taste, and bake in sheets in a rather quick oven, thirty minutes.

Bartlett Cake.

One cup of butter, two of sugar, one of milk, four of flour, four eggs, one wine-glass of whiskey, one cup of currants, one teaspoonful of saleratus, two of cream of tartar. Bake in two loaves in a moderate oven about one hour.

Down East Cake.

One tablespoonful of melted butter, one cup of milk, two of flour, three eggs, one teaspoonful of saleratus, two of cream of tartar. Bake in sheets, in a quick oven, and eat hot with butter.

New York Cup Cake.

One tumbler of butter, two of sugar, four of flour, one of milk, four eggs, one wine-glass of wine, one teaspoonful each of cinnamon, clove, nutmeg, saleratus, and two cups of raisins after they are boiled. Bake in two loaves, in a moderate oven, about an hour.

Champagne Cakes.

One cup of butter, two of sugar, four eggs, one wineglass of champagne, half a teaspoon of saleratus, and flour enough to pat out with the hand. Make into small flat cakes, and bake in a quick oven.

Queen Cake.

One cup of butter, one and a half of sugar, half a pint of milk, one pint of flour, six eggs, one teaspoonful of saleratus, half a pound of currants, lemon. Bake in two loaves, in a moderate oven, nearly an hour.

Loaf Cake.

Two cups of butter, five of sugar, two of sour milk, eight of flour, one teaspoon of saleratus, six eggs. Flavor to taste. This will make four large loaves.

Raisin Cake.

Two thirds of a cup of butter, one and a half of sugar, two thirds of milk, three of flour, one of chopped raisins, three eggs, one teaspoonful of cream of tartar, one half of saleratus. Bake in sheets in a quick oven.

Tumbler Cake.

One tumbler of butter, one of sugar, one of molasses, one of milk, five of flour, four eggs, one teaspoonful of saleratus, two of cream of tartar, spice to taste; one pound of raisins, one of currants, half a pound of citron. Bake in a moderate oven two hours.

Marble Cake.

The White Part. — One half of a cup of butter; one and a half cups of sugar, two of flour, one half cup of milk, the white of four eggs, half a teaspoonful of cream of tartar, one fourth of saleratus. Flavor with lemon.

Dark Part. — One half a cup of butter, one of sugar, one half of molasses, two and a half of flour, one half of milk, the yolks of four and the white of one egg, half a teaspoonful of saleratus, half of cream of tartar, one teaspoonful of cloves, cinnamon, nutmeg, and mace. Drop the white and dark in spoonfuls, alternately. This will make two loaves; bake two hours in a moderate oven.

Composition Cake.

Half a cup of butter, one and a half of sugar, one half of milk, two and a half of flour, three eggs, one teaspoonful of cream of tartar, one half of saleratus, spice, and fruit to your liking. This makes one large loaf. Bake in a moderate oven one hour.

Common Fruit Cake.

One and a half cups of butter, four of sugar, seven and a half of flour, six eggs, one wine-glass of brandy, one tablespoonful of cloves, one of cinnamon, one of nutmeg, one of mace, one of allspice, one teaspoonful of saleratus, and raisins and currants as many as you choose. Bake in a moderate oven two hours or more. This quantity makes three loaves.

Delicate Cake.

Butter the size of an egg, one cup of sugar, one of flour, the whites of five eggs, half a teaspoonful of saleratus, one of cream of tartar. Flavor with bitter almond, and bake in a quick oven.

Ice Cream Cake.

Half a cup of butter, one of sugar, half of milk, two of flour, three eggs, the whites beaten separately, one teaspoonful of cream of tartar, one half of saleratus. Flavor with lemon. Bake in thin sheets in a quick oven. This is nice to eat, while fresh, with ice cream.

Crullers. Mrs. T. Leighton.

A piece of butter the size of an egg, one cup of sugar, one nutmeg, three eggs. Make stiff with flour, and cut in fanciful shapes. Fry in boiling lard.

Fourth of July Cake. Mrs. T. Leighton.

One pound of butter, one of sugar, one of flour, two of currants, one of chopped raisins, one half of citron, one glass of wine or brandy, mace, nutmeg, clove, and lemon, one teaspoonful of saleratus, two of cream of tartar, ten eggs. Bake about two hours and a half in a moderate oven. The quantity will make two loaves. Frost.

Ginger Pound Cak

Two cups of butter, two of sugar, two of molasses, three eggs, nine cups of flour, two tablespoonfuls of ginger, two teaspoonfuls of cinnamon, two of saleratus, one nutmeg. This will make three large loaves.

Pound Cake.

One and a half cups of butter, three of sugar, four of flour, ten eggs, — beat the whites separately, — one teaspoonful of mace. Bake in a rather quick oven forty minutes.

Pound Cake, No. 2.

Two cups of butter, one pint of sugar, one quart of flour, twelve eggs, the yolk of one left out, one teaspoonful of mace. Bake in a rather quick oven forty minutes. Always beat the eggs separately for pound cake, and stir in the whites the last thing.

Wedding Cake.

Two cups of butter, one pint of sugar, one quart of flour, ten eggs, one wine-glass of brandy, one of wine, the rind and juice of one lemon, one tablespoonful of mace, one of cloves, one of cinnamon, one of allspice, half a teaspoonful of saleratus, one of cream of tartar, one pound of raisins, one of currants, half a pound of citron. Bake in a moderate oven three hours. This will make two large loaves.

Gold Cake.

One cup of butter, one pint of sugar, one quart of flour, one teaspoonful of saleratus, two of cream of tartar, the rind and juice of two lemons, the yolks of fourteen eggs. Bake in sheets about two inches deep, in a rather quick oven, and about forty-five minutes.

Golden Cake, No. 2.

Golden cake made the same as the silver, with the yolks of the eggs and half a cup more of flour. Flavor with lemon.

Silver Cake.

One and a half cups of butter, three of sugar, the whites of fourteen eggs, a pint and a half of flour, one teaspoon of saleratus, two of cream of tartar, one teaspoonful bitter almond. Bake in a quick oven, in sheets about two inches deep.

Silver Cake, No. 2.

Half a cup of butter, one of sugar, one half of milk, two of flour, the whites of six eggs, one teaspoonful of cream of tartar, one half of saleratus. Flavor with almond, and bake in sheets in a rather quick oven. Strew in strips of citron.

Sponge Cake.

Beat to a froth seven eggs and two teacups of sugar; stir into this two coffee-cups of flour, in which is mixed one teaspoonful of saleratus and two of cream of tartar. Flavor with the grated rind and juice of one lemon. Bake in sheets in a moderately hot oven. This is very nice.

Sponge Cake, No. 2.

One pint of sugar, one and a half of flour, twelve eggs, one lemon. Beat the sugar, the juice and grated rind of the lemon, and the yolks of the eggs together, then beat the whites to a stiff froth, and add to the mixture; and lastly stir in the flour very lightly. Bake in sheets about half an hour.

Berwick Sponge Cake.

Twenty-five eggs, one pint and a half of sugar, one pint and a half of flour, the grated rind of three and the juice of one lemon. Put together and bake the same as No. 2.

Cocoanut Cake.

One cup of butter, two of sugar, the whites of ten eggs, four cups of flour, one of milk, one cup of prepared cocoanut soaked in the milk, one teaspoonful of saleratus, two of cream of tartar. Bake in sheets in a rather quick oven. If you use the fresh cocoanut, use two cups of it.

Orange Cake.

Beat to a froth four eggs and one and a half cups of sugar; stir into this one *small* cup of cold water, and then two cups of flour, in which are mixed one teaspoonful of cream of tartar, and one half of saleratus. Bake and split the same as cream pies.

Filling for Orange Cake.

Beat to a froth the white of one egg, and mix with it gradually one cup of powdered sugar, and the rind and juice of one orange.

Chocolate Cake.

Make the cake like orange cake. Filling: one quarter of a cake of Baker's chocolate, one half a cup of milk, one of sugar, the whites of two eggs, and a teaspoonful of vanilla. Beat the sugar, chocolate, and eggs together, and stir into the boiling milk; boil until thick, and then add the vanilla.

Chocolate Icing.

Beat to a froth the white of one egg, and then beat in gradually one teacup of powdered sugar, which is mixed with a quarter of a pound of grated chocolate. Flavor with one teaspoonful of vanilla. Split any kind of light cake and spread with jelly; then put on the icing, and set in a warm oven a few minutes to harden.

White Mountain Cake.

Make like Concord cake, and bake in sheets about one inch thick; have all the cakes the same size. Have three cakes in a loaf; lay one cake on a board and spread with frosting; then lay another on top of that, and spread this with frosting; then lay on the third, and frost the whole, and set where it will dry. This is very handsome, and will keep a long time.

Angel Cake.

Take the whites of eleven eggs, and one and one-half cups of granulated sugar, one cup of pastry flour (measure the flour after it has been sifted *four* times), one small teaspoonful of vanilla, one teaspoonful of cream of tartar. Then put in the sieve the flour and cream of tartar, and sift again. Beat the eggs to a stiff froth, beat the sugar into the eggs, and then add the seasoning; add the flour, stirring it in quickly and lightly; beat until you are ready to put it into the oven; put it in a new pan, or a pan that has been used for nothing else, and keep it in a moderate oven forty minutes. Do not grease the pan. When the cake has cooled in the pan, loosen from the sides with a knife, and then take out.

Vanilla Jumbles.

One cup of butter, two of sugar, three eggs, one wine-glass of wine, one spoonful of vanilla, and flour enough to roll out. Roll as thin as the blade of a knife, and cut with an oval cutter. Bake on tin sheets, in a quick oven, until a dark brown. These will keep a year, if kept in a tin box and in a dry place.

PRESERVES.

In making preserves, use a porcelain kettle which should be used for nothing else. Have also a large wooden spoon, which keep expressly for this use. Be very careful not to let the sirup burn or boil over, and always skim carefully. Look at your preserves once a month at least, and if they are beginning to ferment, scald and skim. If they mould on top that will not injure them, but will keep the air from them and thus protect them. Be very careful when removing it not to get any of it in the sirup. Preserves should be kept in a cool, dry place. Always seal them while hot, as by this means you do not seal air in; but if they are allowed to grow cold before sealing they will not keep so well. Heat the jars before putting the preserves in, by setting them in a pan of warm water, and let it heat gradually until it comes to a boiling point. Cut note-paper in round pieces about two inches deeper than the mouth of the jar; make a paste with the white of an egg and a little flour; wet the edges with it and paste on.

Preserved Peaches.

Pare and cut in two peaches that have begun to mellow, but they must be ripe. Take out the stones and then put the fruit in a large earthen dish, cover with coffee crushed sugar. For every pound of fruit allow one pound of sugar. Let this stand over night, and in the morning turn the sirup into the preserving kettle, and clarify; then put in the peaches and cook until tender, which will be in about thirty minutes. Lay them in a stone pot, and pour the boiling sirup over them. When cool, put in small jars, and paste note-paper over the top. Keep in a cool, dry place.

Preserved Pears.

Pare, but do not cut them up. Weigh them, and then boil until tender in just water enough to cover them. When tender, take them out and make a sirup of the water in which they were boiled, and the sugar; allow one pint of water and one pound of sugar to every pound of fruit. Boil this one hour, and then put in the pears and one sliced lemon to every pound; boil gently for forty minutes, then take up, and when cool put in jars. Boil the sirup until thick, and if the jars are stone, pour over the pears while hot.

Crab Apple Preserves.

Wash the apples and drain; leave the stems on them. Make a sirup with the same weight of sugar that you have apples, and half a pint of water to a pound of sugar; simmer the apples in this forty-five minutes, and then take out and lay in a stone jar. Let the sirup simmer one hour longer, and turn boiling on the apples. Seal while hot, with note-paper.

Preserved Pineapple.

Pare and cut the pineapple in slices about an inch thick. Cover with an equal weight of sugar, and let it stand over night. In the morning proceed as with peach preserves.

Preserved Citron Melon.

Pare and cut the melon into handsome pieces about an inch thick. Boil gently until tender, in just water enough to cover it; as soon as it is tender, take out and lay in a platter, and put more on to boil. Do this until all is cooked. Now make a sirup of the weight of the melon in sugar (which weigh before cooking) and the water in which it was boiled. Let this boil one hour; then put in the melon, and one lemon sliced to each pound of melon; a few cloves. Simmer fifty minutes, then take up and boil the sirup half an hour longer, then pour over the melon while hot.

Preserved Apples.

Pare and quarter good tart apples; preserve them the same as melon, omitting the cloves. They are nice to use late in the spring and early in the summer for green apple pies; but as a preserve, they are too insipid.

Preserved Plums.

Take the weight of the plums in sugar, and to two pounds of sugar allow half a pint of water. Make a sirup of this, and when clear, boil the plums in it for forty-five minutes. Do not put many in it at a time. When they are all done, let the sirup boil an hour, and pour over them while hot. Seal with note-paper. This rule will answer for all kinds of plums.

Preserved Cherries.

Cherries are preserved the same as plums.

Preserved Quinces.

Pare, quarter, and cut out the cores. Save the parings and cores for jelly. Preserve the same as pears, omitting the lemon.

Raspberry Jam.

Take equal weights of raspberries and sugar; put the berries in a dish and cover with the sugar, and let them stand over night. In the morning put in the kettle and boil two hours (skimming carefully), and put up in jars; seal with note paper. Strawberries and blackberries are cooked in the same manner.

Barberries Preserved with Pears.

Weigh the barberries, and make a sirup of an equal weight of sugar, allowing half a pint of water to a pound of sugar. When the sirup is clear, put in the barberries (which must be free from stems), and boil fifty minutes

When the barberries are all cooked, put as many pears, pared and quartered, as you have barberries into the sirup, and boil until tender; then take up and put with the barberries. Boil the sirup thirty minutes, and then pour boiling over the fruit.

Barberries Preserved in Molasses.

One peck of barberries, six quarts of molasses. Pick the barberries free from stems and imperfect ones. Let the molasses come to a boil, then put in the barberries, and boil about fifty minutes. They will be clear and full when done. Skim them out and put in the jars. Save two quarts of the sirup for drinks, and turn the remainder over the barberries. Be very careful that the molasses shall not burn. Sweet apples may be cooked with these in the same manner that pears are cooked with those done in sugar.

Grape Marmalade.

Put the grapes in a stone pot, and set the pot into a kettle with cold water; set this on the fire and boil until the grapes will mash easily; stir them often, and jam with bowl of the spoon. Take them up and strain through a sieve. To a quart of the pulp allow a pint of sugar, and boil forty minutes.

Currant Jelly.

To be nice the currants must be *just ripe*, and neither more nor less. Put them, stems and all, into a stone pot and cover to keep the steam in. Set the pot into a kettle with cold water, and place on the fire. Boil until they will all jam easily. Jam them with the bowl of the spoon. Lay a piece of thin muslin in a sieve, and turn the currants into it; squeeze the juice through. If you are careful to have it clear now, you will not have to strain it after the sugar is added. To a pint of juice add a pint of sugar, and boil fifty minutes. Take it off the fire and let it stand until so cool that it will not break the glasses, but no longer, and then fill the glasses; let them stand in the sun a few days, and them seal with note-paper.

Currant Shrub.

Make the same as jelly but boil only ten minutes When cool, bottle. Raspberry, strawberry, and blackberry shrubs made in the same way.

Apple Jelly.

Make the same as quince, with the addition of a stick of cinnamon and one lemon to a quart of juice, after the sugar is added. It will take longer to cook than quince.

Quince Jelly.

Put the cores and parings in the preserving kettle, and cover with cold water. Boil gently two hours; then squeeze through a thick piece of cloth, and to a pint of juice allow a pint of sugar. Boil until it will jelly when a little is put in a saucer, then treat as currant jelly. Where water is put with fruit you cannot limit the time of boiling.

To Can Berries.

Put the berries in a nice tin pan, and set over a boiler of boiling water, and to a gallon of berries allow one cup of boiling water; heat the berries to a boiling point. (Cover them, and stir occasionally, and they will heat much sooner.) Heat self-sealing jars by putting them in a pan of cold water. Set on the stove, and let the water boil; now fill the jars to the top, and put on the covers, and set up; as the glass is expanded by the heat, they cannot be set tight now; but after they become cool, get a man to set them up very tight. Set away in a cool, dry place. Always use the fruit as soon as opened. If these directions are followed, you may put up any kind of fruit, and keep it nice for years.

PICKLES.

Pickled Cucumbers.

PICK the cucumbers before they get very large; lay them in a tub, and cover with a boiling brine of one gill of salt to one gallon of water; let this stand until cold, and then turn the brine back into the kettle and boil again, and pour over the cucumbers; do this five times, and then turn off and cover with boiling alum water (allow one heaping spoonful of alum to one gallon of water). When cold, turn off, and boil again, and turn on the cucumbers a second time. When this is cold turn off, and drain the cucumbers Now put on a few quarts of good cider vinegar in a porcelain kettle, and when it boils, drop a few cucumbers in at a time, and let them boil about eight minutes; then skim out and drain. Do this until they are all scalded. Lay them in a stone pot and cover with good cider vinegar. You may use bell peppers and spice if you choose. You cannot fail to have good pickles if you follow this rule.

Tomato Pickles.

Cut green tomatoes into slices about an inch thick, and sprinkle with salt. (Allow half a cup of salt to a peck of tomatoes), and let them stand over night. In the morning turn off all the liquor and scald them in boiling vinegar; then lay them in the stone pots and sprinkle between them half a spoonful of white mustard seed and a handful of whole cloves. Cover with cold vinegar.

Tomato Pickles, No. 2.

Cut a peck of green tomatoes in slices, and lay in a stone jar; cover with one pint of molasses. Skim when it ferments, and your pickles are made. This is *good*.

Piccalilli.

Slice one peck of tomatoes and sprinkle with one handful of salt; let them stand over night, and in the morning turn off the liquor. Chop the tomatoes, one cabbage-head, seven onions, and four green peppers. Mix with this half a pint of whole mustard, half a teacup of sugar, half a teacupful of horseradish, and vinegar enough to cover the whole. Stew until soft.

Tomato Catsup.

Cut up one gallon of ripe tomatoes, and put on in a porcelain kettle and boil. Prepare half a pint of sugar, half a pint of strong cider vinegar, or more if not strong; one tablespoonful of salt, one teaspoonful of cloves, one of allspice, one quarter of a teaspoonful of cayenne pepper. Boil the tomatoes half an hour and then run them through a sieve. Now put them on with the spice, vinegar, and sugar, and boil until there is about two quarts and a pint. Cool and bottle.

SAUCES.

Drawn Butter.

BEAT one cup of butter and two spoonfuls of flour to a cream, and pour over this one pint of boiling water. Set on the fire and let it come to boil, but do *not boil* Serve immediately.

Egg Sauce.

Chop up two hard boiled eggs, and stir into drawn butter.

Oyster Sauce.

Set a basin on the fire with half a pint of oysters and one pint of boiling water; let them boil three minutes, and then stir in half a cup of butter beaten to a cream, with two spoonfuls of flour; let this come to a boil, and serve.

Celery Sauce.

Chop fine two heads of celery, and boil one hour; at the end of that time, have about a pint and a half of water with it, and stir in two spoonfuls of flour wet with cold water. Boil this ten minutes, and then stir in two spoonfuls of butter. Season with pepper and salt, and serve.

SAUCES.

Caper Sauce.

Into a pint of drawn butter stir three spoonfuls of capers.

Mint Sauce.

Chop fine half a cupful of mint, and add to it a cup of vinegar and a spoonful of sugar.

Bread Sauce.

Half a pint of grated bread crumbs, one pint of milk, and one onion. Boil this until the sauce is smooth, then take out the onion and stir in two spoonfuls of butter, and salt and pepper. Boil up once, and serve.

Coddled Apples.

Pare and core with an apple-corer, cook the same as for apple-sauce; but allow one pint of sugar to one quart of water.

Cranberry Sauce.

Pick and wash the cranberries, and put in the preserving kettle with half a pint of water to one quart of berries; now put the sugar on top of the berries, allowing a pint of sugar to a quart of berries. Set on the fire and stew about half an hour. Stir often to prevent burning. They will not need straining, and will preserve their rich color cooked in this way. Never cook cranberries before putting in the sugar. Less sugar may be used if you do not wish them very rich.

Apple Sauce.

Pare, quarter, and core nice tart apples Make a sirup of two quarts of water and one cup of sugar; simmer the apples in this until tender, but do not break them; then lay in an earthen dish; do this until they are all cooked. (Do not put many in the sirup at a time), and then let the sirup get cool, and turn on the apples.

Baked Pears.

Put the pears in a deep earthen dish or a baking-pan, and to a dozen good-sized pears allow half a cup of sugar and a pint and a half of water. Bake in a moderate oven two hours and a half or three. They will not keep many days cooked in this manner, but they are nice. Sweet apples are cooked in the same manner.

Stewed Prunes.

Wash the prunes in warm water and rub them well between the hands. Put them in a kettle that you can cover tight, with two quarts of water to one of prunes. Stew them gently two hours. These will not keep more than two days in warm weather, but cooked in this way they do not require any sugar, and are very nice.

Dried Apple Sauce.

Pick and wash the apples carefully, then place in a

preserving kettle. For one pint of dried apple cut the thin yellow skin off a lemon, and then pare and cut up the inside. Put the yellow skin (be careful not to get any of the white) and the inside into the kettle with the apple, and three pints of cold water. Cover tight, and simmer three hours, then put in one pint of sugar, but do not stir the apple, and simmer two hours longer. *Never stir* dried apple-sauce.

DRINKS.

Tea.

SCALD the teapot and put in the tea, allowing one teaspoonful to each person; pour over this half a cup of *boiling* water (soft water is the best), and steep in a hot place, but not where it will boil, ten minutes; then turn in all the boiling water you wish, and serve.

Coffee.

Put one cup of ground coffee and one pint of cold water into the coffee-pot; set the pot on the fire and boil ten minutes after it comes to a boil; then turn in a pint of boiling water and a piece of salt fish skin about an inch square. Boil ten minutes longer, then turn in half a cup of cold water and set one side five minutes; turn into another pot, and send to the table. Always serve boiled milk with coffee.

Shells.

Put one quart of cold water and half a cup of shells into the pot, and boil gently four or five hours; add boiling water occasionally. About twenty minutes before serving, add one pint of new milk and boiling water enough to make three pints in all; let this boil a few minutes, strain and serve.

Chocolate.

With four spoonfuls of grated chocolate mix one of sugar, and wet with one of *boiling* water. Rub this smooth with the bowl of the spoon, and then stir into one pint of boiling water; let this boil up once, and then add one pint of good milk; let this boil up once, and serve.

Prepared Cocoa.

Prepared cocoa is made the same as chocolate, omitting the sugar. All milk may be used if preferred. Never boil chocolate or prepared cocoa more than one minute. Boiling makes it oily. The quicker it is used after making the better.

EGGS.

Boiled Eggs.

PUT the eggs in a tin basin and pour boiling water over them; let them stand on a part of the stove where they will keep hot, but not boil, for ten minutes, or boil in boiling water three minutes and a half. The first method is the best. This is for rare done eggs.

Fried Eggs.

Have boiling lard in the frying pan; break the eggs into a saucer one at a time, and slide them gently into the pan; now, with a large spoon, dip the boiling lard and pour it over the eggs; do this until they are set, then dish.

Dropped Eggs.

Turn a quart of boiling water into a basin with one spoonful of salt. Break the eggs, one at a time, into a saucer; dip one side of the saucer into the water and let the eggs slide gently into it. Boil gently until set, which will be in about two minutes, and serve on toast.

Poached Eggs.

Break and beat up two eggs, and stir into them two tablespoonfuls of milk and half a teaspoonful of salt; put them into a basin, with half a spoonful of butter, and set over the fire. Stir until it thickens, and then serve.

Scrabbled Eggs.

Beat together four eggs, and then turn into a pan with one spoonful of melted butter. Stir quickly over a hot fire one minute, and serve.

Omelets.

Beat lightly two eggs, and stir in one spoonful of milk and a pinch of salt. Heat the omelet pan hot, and then put in a little bit of butter, and when melted turn in the beaten eggs; set on the fire, shake the pan, cook until a light brown; then fold the omelet and serve on a hot dish. Ham, mushroom, lobster, chicken, and all kinds of omelets are made by chopping up the meat, and laying it between the folds before dishing.

MISCELLANEOUS RECEIPTS.

Buttered Toast.

BEAT to a froth one cup of butter and three tablespoonfuls of flour; pour over this one pint and a half of *boiling* water; set this over a kettle of boiling water for ten minutes. Cut bread in slices half an inch thick; toast brown and dip into this. Serve very hot.

Milk Toast.

Put one quart of milk in a tin pail or basin, and set into a kettle of boiling water. When it comes to a boil stir in two spoonfuls of flour, mixed with half a cup of milk, one spoonful of butter, and salt to taste; let this boil ten minutes, and then put in the bread, which must be toasted brown. Cook five minutes longer and serve.

French Toast.

Soak bakers' bread, as for Italian fritters; toast brown, butter and serve hot.

Sandwiches.

Take the pieces of ham which are left on the bone after all the slices are cut off and chop rather fine. Cut bread into thin slices (the milk yeast is the best for this) and butter. Now spread with the ham, and lay another buttered slice over this. Trim the edges. This is a very nice dish for evening parties or picnics. Fold them in a damp towel until they are sent to the table. They may be made by putting slices of cold ham, tongue, beef, or chicken between the slices of buttered bread.

Oyster Stew.

Drain all the liquor from the oysters; put it into a porcelain kettle, and let it come to a boil; then skim off all the scum. Now turn in the milk, which you have let come to a boil in hot water. (Allow one quart of milk to one pint of oysters.) Stir in also one spoonful of butter or more, salt and pepper to taste. Now put in the oysters, let them boil up once, and serve with a dish of oyster crackers.

Corn Starch Cakes.

One cup of butter, one and a half of sugar, one and a half of flour, one half of corn starch, one half of milk, four eggs, one teaspoonful of cream of tartar, one half of saleratus. Flavor with lemon. Bake in sheets. This will make two sheets, and will keep a month.

Seed Cakes.

Butter the size of an egg, two cups of sugar, and four of flour, half a teaspoonful of saleratus, and milk to wet it so that it will roll easily; seeds to taste. Roll about half an inch thick, and bake in a quick oven.

Strawberry Short Cake.

Two cups of flour, one cup of sour milk, butter the size of a walnut, one third of a teaspoonful of soda, one fourth of a teaspoonful of salt; mix lightly, and bake in a quick oven. While baking take one pint and a half of strawberries, and mash fine. When the cake is baked, cut in two, and butter each part; then put on the larger portion a layer of sugar, and then strawberries, then a layer of sugar, then lay on the other part, and serve immediately.

Cream Cakes.

Turn on one cup of butter, one pint of *boiling* water. Stir two good-sized cups of flour into this, then take off and cool. When cool, stir in five well-beaten eggs Drop on tins and bake.

FILLING. — Make the filling as for cream pies. It will take twice the quantity.

Tapioca Cream.

Four large spoonfuls of tapioca, just cover with cold water, and soak over night. Set one quart of milk on the fire to warm. Beat the yolks of four eggs and one cup of sugar together. Stir into the boiling milk, with a pinch of salt, and then stir in the tapioca. Beat the whites to a stiff froth and stir into the custard, then turn into a dish. Flavor with lemon or vanilla. Cook like a soft custard before adding the whites.

Cider Cake.

One cup of butter, two of sugar, four of flour, three eggs, half a pint of cider, one teaspoonful of soda, spice to taste.

Veal Loaf.

Take three and a half pounds of veal from the leg and chop it very fine; add six powdered crackers, half a pound of salt pork chopped fine, and two eggs well-beaten. Season with tablespoonful of salt, one teaspoonful black pepper, half a teaspoonful of allspice, one half of ground clove, half a small onion chopped fine; sage or sweet marjorum may be used instead of onion if preferred. Knead all this together and make it into a loaf, and place it on a tin sheet. Beat one egg, and pour it over the loaf; put bits of butter on the top, and sift over it half a pound of crackers. Take half a teacup of hot water, add a piece of butter the size of a nutmeg, and with this baste the loaf three or four times while baking. Bake two hours. When cold cut in thin slices, and serve for either breakfast or tea.

Lemon Pies.

Take two lemons and grate away the outside, and not use it. Chop the rest very fine; into two teacups of hot water, stir two spoonfuls of corn starch, and boil; add two teacups of sugar; when cool, add the beaten yolks of four eggs and the chopped lemon; stir well together. Line two plates, and pour in the mixture and bake. Beat the whites of the eggs to a froth with six tablespoonfuls of sugar. Spread this over the pies; set in the oven again and bake a light brown.

Hop Yeast.

Extra nice. Into one quart of water in which potatoes have been boiled put a pinch of hops, and boil a few minutes; strain, and then stir in one spoonful of sugar and one of salt. Let this cool, and when blood warm add half a cup of good yeast. It soon foams up like beer, and will keep in all temperatures. Put *nothing* in the yeast but the potato water, hops, sugar, salt, and the rising.

Baked Buckwheat Cakes.

Mix and rise the buckwheat over night, as for griddle cakes, only a little stiffer; in the morning heat French roll pans very hot in the oven; grease them, turn in the batter, and bake.

Frosting.

Beat to a froth the white of one egg. Beat into it, very gradually, one teacup of powdered sugar, and one scant tablespoonful of corn starch, and the juice of one lemon. Spread this over the cake, then wet a clean knife in cold water and smooth the frosting with it. Set in a warm, dry place to harden.

Frosting, No. 2.

Take about one sixteenth part of an ounce of gelatine and put in a bowl; just moisten with cold water, and let it stand half an hour; then pour on it *boiling* water enough to dissolve; now stir in powdered sugar enough to thicken. Season with lemon, and spread on the cake. This is not so handsome as that made with the white of an egg, but is made quickly, and will harden in half an hour. Frost the cake while it is warm, as it dries more quickly and adheres better.

Whitpot Pudding.

One cup of Indian meal, one of molasses, a little salt. Scald thoroughly with boiling water. Add a quart of milk; pour into the baking-dish and bake one hour, *stirring thoroughly at least twice while it is baking.* Let it get about half cool before you serve it.

Boiled Indian Pudding.

Four cups of Indian meal, one cup of beef suet chopped fine, one cup of molasses, a little salt. Pour on boiling water enough to make a thick batter. Boil in a cloth, tied very loosely, two hours or more. Put in the pot before the water quite boils. Serve with butter and sirup.

Spiced Currants.

Five pounds of currants, four pounds of sugar, one pint of vinegar, two tablespoonfuls of cloves, two of cinnamon. Stew half an hour. To eat with roast meat.

Chili Sauce.

Take nine large or eighteen small tomatoes, scald, peel, and chop, with two peppers and one large onion. Add one tablespoonful of salt, two of sugar, one teaspoonful each of ginger, cloves, allspice, cinnamon, one nutmeg, and two small cups of vinegar. Stew half an hour; bottle while hot.

Graham Pies.   Mrs. C. Thaxter.

Into a pint of Graham flour, stir one teaspoonful of salt; wet with boiling water enough to make a stiff paste. Roll this very thin, and cut into cakes about three inches in diameter; put into these a spoonful of apple-sauce and fold them. Bake on tin sheets. These can be eaten by any dyspeptic.

REMARKS ON DIGESTION.

In the stomach is produced a liquid secretion called the gastric juice. This does not act upon starch or fat of any kind. The only thing it dissolves is the albuminous matter. Now, when this albuminous matter is not saturated with fat, the gastric juice acts upon it readily; but, as in the case of pastry, doughnuts, fried meats, etc., where the whole mass is saturated with a fatty substance, it takes a long time before the gastric juice can get at the albuminous matter to act upon it; hence the distress by the over working of the stomach; and, if this kind of food is partaken of frequently, the stomach force will be weakened, and refuse to do its work. This will disarrange every other member of the digestive organs; and, in a short time, you have a first-class dyspeptic. All food, therefore, should be as light, porus, and free from fat as possible.

When fat is used, it should be in such a manner that it will separate readily from the other substances on entering the stomach. Alcohol retards digestion, and renders it incomplete, by coagulating the gastric juice. Food, when taken into the stomach either *very* hot or *very* cold, does not digest readily. Food taken when the body or mind is very tired does not digest readily. Digestion goes on very slowly during sleep; but it is more complete, and repairs the waste of the body more thoroughly than the rapid digestion of the walking hours. Children digest food more rapidly than adults, and should therefore be given a light lunch, when more than four hours intervene between the regular meals.

It is a great mistake to think that light breakfasts are better than substantial ones. The breakfast supplies the fuel for the great waste which goes on during the busiest part of the day, and therefore should be of a simple, nutritious character, and an abundant supply of it. Another mistake made by many persons is the taking of a number of hours of exercise before breakfast.

The stomach, while empty, is in a condition to receive disease. In a high, dry atmosphere, there is less danger from this habit; but in a country which is at all malarious, it is one of the most dangerous things which can be done.

Regularity as to the time of eating is also one of the necessary things to be observed, that the digestion may be perfect. Pastry should be used very sparingly, puddings, fruit, and light deserts taking the place of pies

The preparation of food should be made more a matter of conscience, with the housekeeper and cook, than it is at present. In planning the preparation of a dish, the question should not be, Is it convenient, and will it please? but, Will it be healthful, mentally, morally, and physically? for the food we eat affects all three natures.

Then food, to do its highest and best work, must be of the best quality, prepared carefully (but always to retain its simplest form), partaken of regularly in a cheerful room and in cheerful company.

MEDICINAL.

Unfailing Cure for Constipation.

THREE teacupfuls of coarse, clean wheat-bran, three of sifted flour, one heaping teaspoonful of cream-tartar, one-half of soda, one of salt. seven of sweet butter. Mix with cold milk, and roll into thin biscuit; and bake thoroughly in a moderately hot oven. They should be from one fourth to one-third of an inch thick, and be cut with a small biscuit-cutter.

Great care must be taken that they do not burn, and at the same time that they get *thoroughly baked*. They will keep a long time if kept in a tight tin box; and they should be eaten at each meal. — *From Mr. Leonard Scott, after twenty years' experience.*

Cure, No. 2.

A little while before retiring, mix a tablespoonful of flaxseed in cold water enough to make it pour readily, and, on going to bed, drink this. It is not nauseating at all, and will act on the bowels without deranging them as drugs always do.

Drinking a glass of cold water at night and in the morning helps many persons. Eating fruit is also good.

Persons having this trouble should eat vegetables, meats, hominy, oatmeal, and coarse breads. They should also take a great deal of exercise.

Diarrhœa.

Brown rice as you would the coffee bean, and then either grind or mash in the mortar; take half a cup of the ground rice, and pour about a quart of boiling water over it and let it stand about ten or fifteen minutes; then strain and sweeten with loaf sugar and season with boiled milk. Drink of this freely. This is particularly nice for children.

Cure No. 2.—Flour Gruel.

Let one quart of fresh milk come to a boil, and then stir in one tablespoonful of flour, which has been mixed with milk enough to make a smooth paste; boil this mixture thirty minutes, being careful not to let it burn. Season with salt and strain. The patient should be kept warm and quiet.

Inflammation of the Bowels.

Cover the bowels with thin slices of fresh beef, and, when they begin to grow dark, remove them and put on more fresh beef; continue this until the inflammation is all drawn out.

Burns.

Wet saleratus and spread on a cloth; bind this around the burnt part, and, in few hours, it will be nearly well, unless the burn is very deep, in which case the saleratus should be removed; and after being removed the burn should be covered with a piece of old linen on which has been rubbed a little mutton tallow or sweet oil.

Neuralgia.

One of the causes of neuralgia is constipation; and therefore one of the first things to do is to get the bowels in a healthy condition.

A poultice made from the common white bean is a great relief. Boil the beans in water enough to make a thick paste; mash them, and spread the paste thickly on a cloth: then cover the paste with a thin piece of muslin, and bind on the painful parts. The bean poultice will retain heat longer than one made of any thing else; and, as heat and moisture opens the pores, it thus relieves the pain. Hot oatmeal gruel heats the system quickly and thoroughly, for which reason it should be taken freely in all cases of colds, neuralgia, and rheumatism.

Growing-in-Nails.

When the nails are trimmed cut a deep place in the centre of any that have a tendency to grow into the flesh. The inclination of the parts of the nail to grow together will keep it out of the flesh.

Nosebleed.

Roll a piece of soft paper quite hard, and pack hard between the upper lip and gum, and in a few minutes the bleeding will stop.

Cure for Hoarseness.

Bake a lemon or sour orange for twenty minutes in a moderate oven; then open it at one end, and dig out the inside, which sweeten with sugar or molasses,. and eat. This will cure hoareness and remove pressure from the lungs.

Under the heading of "Medicinal" I do not give any rules that will take the place of a physician in cases of severe sickness; but I give simple remedies which have been *thoroughly tested*, and which I hope may relieve many others by being thus made public.

MISCELLANEOUS.

Mock Bisque Soup. — Very nice.

STEW one can of tomatoes (one quart can). While the tomatoes are stewing, put three pints of milk on to boil, setting the basin in which the milk is into another of hot water. When the milk comes to a boil, stir in a tablespoonful of flour, which has been thoroughly mixed with a little cold milk. Let this boil ten minutes, and then add butter the size of an egg, salt and pepper to taste. The tomatoes, which were put on at the same time with the milk, are now ready to strain into the mixture. Just before straining, stir a pinch of saleratus into the tomatoes to remove the acidity. Serve immediately.

Chicken Pillau, — A Southern Dish.

Cut a chicken into pieces the size you wish to serve at table, then wash clean and put into the stewpan with about one-eighth of a pound of salt pork, which has been cut up into small pieces. Cover this with cold water, and boil gently until the chicken begins to grow tender, which will be in about one hour, unless the chicken is old. Now season the liquor and chicken with salt and pepper, rather highly, and add three teacups of rice, which has been picked and washed, and let it boil thirty or forty minutes longer.

There should be a good quart of liquor in the stewpan when the rice is added. Care must be taken that it does not burn. Pork or any other kind of meat can be used.

To Pickle Oysters.

Two hundred large oysters, one half pint of vinegar, one-half pint of white-wine, four spoonfuls of salt, six spoonfuls of whole black pepper, and a little mace. Strain the liquor, and add the aboved-named ingredients, then put on the fire and boil up, and pour while boiling hot over the oysters, and let them stand ten minutes: then pour the liquor off them and let both oysters and liquor get cold; then put the oysters in a jar with the liquor, and cover tight. They will keep some time.

Oatmeal.

Oatmeal, Indian meal, and hominy all require two things to make them perfect: that is, *plenty of water* when first put on to boil, and a *long* time to boil.

Have about two quarts of boiling water in a large stewpan, and into it stir one cup of oatmeal, which you have already wet with cold water; boil this an hour, stirring often, and then add half a spoonful of salt and boil an hour longer. If it should get too stiff add more boiling water; or, if too thin, boil a little longer: you cannot boil it too much.

The only trouble there is in cooking oatmeal is that it takes a long time, and surely no one will let that stand in the way when it is so much better for having the extra time. It is also very necessary that there be an abundance of water to begin with; if not, it will never be as good, no matter how much may be added after it has been cooking any time.

Hominy.

Wash in two waters one cup of hominy, then stir it into one quart of boiling water with a little salt, and boil from thirty to sixty minutes: it is better boiled sixty than thirty. Be careful that it does not burn. Hominy can be used more than oatmeal, as it can be eaten with any kind of meat, and should be cooked once a day. It is nice and appropriate for any meal. It is also good eaten warm or cold with milk.

Hominy Griddle-cakes.

To one pint of warm, boiled hominy add a pint of milk or water, and flour enough to make a thin batter; beat up two or three eggs, and stir them into the batter with a little salt. Fry as any other griddle-cake. They are delicious.

Waffles.

One pint of sifted flour, milk enough to make a thin

batter, which will be about two-thirds of a pint, a small piece of butter melted (about a tablespoonful after being melted), two eggs beaten very light, a little salt. Mix the milk with the flour gradually until it is a smooth paste, then the salt and melted butter, and last the well-beaten eggs. Have the waffle-irons about as hot as a griddle for cakes, and butter them well. Pour in enough of the batter to cover the iron, and put the other side down gently on it. Let it stand over the fire about thirty seconds, and then turn over and let the other side remain to the fire the same time, then remove and place where they will keep warm until there are enough cooked to serve.

Many persons butter the waffles as they place them on the dish, and others add sugar. It is very well to do so if that is known to be the taste of all the family; but it is always safe to let people do those things at the table.

Waffles can be made with batters — given under the rules for bread, rice, and Indian griddle-cakes, also hominy.

Togus Bread.

Three cups of sweet milk and one of sour, three cups of Indian meal and one of flour, one half-cup of molasses, one teaspoonful of saleratus, salt. Steam three hours.

Bread made with Yeast-cakes.

For two quarts of flour, take one good sized yeast-cake, and break up in one pint of blood-warm water; stir until it is thoroughly softened, then from your two quarts of flour take enough to make a thin batter, and set where it will keep warm for about two hours. If the yeast is good, it will be a sponge in that time. Now, take the remainder of your flour, and proceed as for "Bread No. 2," in the first part of the book, of course omitting the flour and water, and using only half as much salt and sugar.

Cake without Eggs.

Four cups of flour, two of sugar, one and a half of boiled milk, one of butter (melted in the milk while boiling), one teaspoonful of cream-tartar, one-half of saleratus. Spice to taste.

Kneaded Plum Cake.

Two and a half cups of sugar, one-half of butter, one-half of sour milk, two spoonfuls of cream, one teaspoonful of saleratus, one-half of cinnamon, one-half of nutmeg, one cup of chopped raisins, and flour enough to knead. Roll an inch thick, and cut into oblong pieces. Bake on sheets in a quick oven.

Soft Gingerbread.

Six teacups of flour, three of molasses, one of cream, one of lard or butter, two eggs, one teaspoonful of saleratus, ginger. Excellent.

Molasses Pound Cake.

One quart of molasses, one pint of water, six and a half pints of flour, one ounce of soda, one-half of alum, one heaping cup of butter, six eggs, one ounce of cinnamon, one pound of raisins. Boil the alum in part of the pint of water and let cool before mixing it with the other ingredients.

Instead of the alum, one-ounce of cream-tartar may be used.

Hard Gingerbread.

Very nice. One cup of sugar, one of butter, one-third of molasses, one-half of sour milk or cream, one teaspoonful of saleratus, one tablespoonful of ginger, flour enough to roll. Roll thin, and cut in oblong pieces, and bake quickly. Care must be taken that there is not too much flour mixed in with the dough. All kinds of cakes that are rolled should have no more flour, than is absolutely necessary to work it.

Jumbles.

Three cups of sugar, two of butter, five of flour, one egg, half a teaspoonful of soda, flavor to taste. Roll thin, sprinkle with sugar, and cut with a cutter that will take a piece from the centre. Bake in a quick oven.

Seed Cakes.

Three-fourths of a pint of sugar, one cup of butter,

one quart and half a pint of flour, one teaspoonful of saleratus, two eggs, seeds. Roll thin, cut into round cakes, and bake quickly.

Cookies.

One cup of butter, two of sugar, five of flour, one teaspoonful of saleratus dissolved in four of milk, one egg, flavor to taste. Roll and bake as seed-cakes.

Shrewsbury Cake.

Two cups of butter, one pint of sugar, three pints of flour, four eggs, one-half a tablespoonful of mace. Roll thin, cut into small cakes, and bake in a quick oven. There must not be a grain more flour used than what is given in the rule. The room that they are made in must be rather cool, and they cannot be made in very warm weather. They will keep a long time, and are perfectly delicious.

Sponge Rusk.

Two cups of sugar, one of butter, two of milk, one of yeast, three eggs. Rub butter, sugar, and eggs together, add milk and yeast and flour enough to make a thick batter. Let it stand in a warm place until it is light, then add flour enough to make as thick as for biscuit, and then shape and put in the pan in which it is to be baked, and let it stand two or three hours (three hours unless it is very warm weather), and bake in a moderate oven about forty minutes.

It is always best to set the sponge at night and then it will be ready to bake in the forenoon. If you want them warm for tea, of course you must set your sponge early in the morning.

Cocoanut Drops.

Beat the whites of four eggs with half a pint of powdered sugar, stir with these ingredients one grated cocoanut; bake in small cakes in a moderate oven.

Prepare the pan for them as for kisses.

Railroad Cake.

Two cups of sugar, two of flour, six tablespoonfuls of butter, two of milk, six eggs, one teaspoonful of saleratus, two of cream-tartar, lemon peel. Bake in shallow pans in a quick oven.

Regatta Cake.

Two pounds of raised dough, one pint of sugar, one cup of butter, four eggs, one nutmeg, one glass of wine, one teaspoonful of saleratus, one pound of raisins. Mix thoroughly, and put in deep pans which have been thoroughly greased, and let rise half an hour if very warm weather, and three-quarters if in cold weather. Bake in a moderate oven.

Federal Cake.

One pint of sugar, one and a half cups of butter, three

pints of flour, four eggs, two wineglasses of milk, two of wine, two of brandy, one teaspoonful of cream-tartar, one half of saleratus, fruit and spice to your taste.

Bake in deep pans; the time of baking will depend upon how much fruit is used.

Loaf Cake.

Two quarts of sugar, seven cups of butter, six quarts of sifted flour, six pounds of fruit, one pint of wine, one pint of yeast, eight nutmegs, mace, twelve eggs, one quart of milk. It may be made at such a time of day (being governed by the weather) as will give it time to get perfectly light by evening.

Put in half the butter and half the eggs, the milk, flour, and yeast, and beat up thoroughly. In the evening add the remainder of the butter, rubbing it with the sugar, eggs, and spice.

Let it rise again, until morning; then add the fruit, and put it in deep pans and let rise about half an hour.

Bake, in a slow oven, from two to three hours.

Queen's Cake.

One cup of butter, one pint of sugar, one quart of flour, four eggs, half a gill of wine, half of brandy, half of thin cream, one pound of fruit, spice to taste.

Warm the wine, brandy, and cream together, and stir quickly into the beaten sugar, butter, and eggs; add the fruit the last thing.

Bake in deep pans in a moderate oven.

Wedding Cake.

Nine cups of butter, five pints of sugar, four quarts of flour, sixty eggs, seven pounds of currants, three and a half of citron, four of shelled almonds, seven of raisins, one and a half pints of brandy, two ounces of mace To be mixed and baked like wedding cake in the first part of the book. This will make eight loaves, and will keep for years.

Black Cake.

Three cups of butter, one quart of sugar, three pints of flour, half a pint of molasses, half a pint of brandy, half a pint of wine, one teaspoonful of saleratus, one ounce each of all kinds of spice, twelve eggs, three pounds of raisins, two of currants, one-half a pound of citron.

Bake in deep pans, in a moderate oven, between three and four hours. This is one of the finest rules for rich cake in the book.

Caramel Frosting.

One cup of brown sugar, and one square of Baker's Chocolate scraped fine, one tablespoonful of water. Simmer gently, being careful not to let it burn, twenty minutes. Spread on the cake while hot.

Glacie Cake.

Make rich cup-cake and bake in sheets. When nearly cold, frost with the following preparation : Wet with cold water a *small* pinch of Cox's Sparkling Gelatine. When ready to frost the cake, dissolve this in about one-fourth of a wineglass of *boiling* water, and then thicken with powdered sugar; flavor with lemon, and spread on the cake. This will harden in fifteen or twenty minutes, and cuts nicely the first day, but is not so good to keep as that made with the white of egg.

Golden Frosting.

Into the yolks of two eggs stir powdered sugar enough to thicken, and flavor strong with lemon. This does not have as good a flavor as the other kinds, but it makes a change.

Chocolate Pies.

Make plain cup-cake and bake in Washington-pie plates, having the cakes thick enough to split. Split them and spread one-half with the following filling, then place the top piece on and sprinkle with powdered sugar :—

Filling for Chocolate Pies.

One square of Baker's Chocolate, one cup of sugar, the yolks of two eggs, and one-third of a cup of boiling milk. Mix scraped chocolate and sugar together, then add, very slowly, the boiling milk, then the eggs and simmer about ten minutes, taking care not to burn the mixture. Flavor with vanilla. Have perfectly cold before using. The cake must always be fresh.

Sweet-Potato Pie.

When the potatoes are dry and mealy, one quart of the potato after it has been pared, boiled, and mashed, one quart of milk, four eggs, salt, nutmeg, cinnamon, and sugar to sweeten to taste. Bake the same as squash pies. If the potatoes are very moist, use less milk.

English Plum Pudding.

One pound of suet chopped fine, one pint of sugar, one pound of stale grated bread, one pound of raisins, two of currants, one glass of brandy, two teaspoonfuls of ginger, two nutmegs, half a pint of milk, a little salt. Beat well and steam five hours. Serve with rich sauce.

Eve's Pudding.

Six eggs, six apples, six ounces of bread, six ounces of sugar, six ounces of currants; salt and nutmeg. Boil three hours or steam four. Serve with wine sauce.

Amherst Pudding.

Three-fourths of a cup of butter, three-fourths of a

pint of sugar, four eggs. five tablespoonfuls strained apple grated peel and juice of one lemon, nutmeg and rose-water, if you like. Bake in a shallow pudding-dish which has been lined with rich paste rolled very thin. Let it become partly cooled before it is served.

Carrot Pudding.

Twenty carrots boiled and strained, two cups of butter, one pint of sugar, the yolks of twelve and whites of six eggs, one nutmeg, half a pint of wine, one pint of milk. Bake like Amherst pudding.

Down-East Pudding.

One pint of molasses, one quart of flour, one tablespoonful of salt, one teaspoonful of soda, three pints of blackberries Boil three hours, and serve with sauce made in the following manner:—

One teacup of powdered sugar, one-half of butter, one egg, two teaspoonfuls of *boiling* water, and one of brandy. Beat the butter to a cream, and then add very gradually the sugar beat in the yolk of the egg, and, when perfectly creamy, add the white, which has been beaten to a froth, then add the water and stir it very carefully. The brandy should be beaten with the butter and sugar.

Rachel Pudding.

One quart of bread crumbs, one of apples, cut up very

fine, half a cup of suet, which has been chopped very fine, one cup of English currants, rind and juice of two lemons, four eggs well beaten. Mix thoroughly, grease a pudding-mould, and put in the mixture. Steam three hours. Serve with rich wine sauce.

Princess Pudding.

One box of Cox's Sparkling Gelatine. Soak one hour in one pint of cold water, and then add one pint of *boiling* water, and one pint of wine, the juice of four lemons, and three large cups of sugar. Beat the whites of four eggs to a stiff froth, and stir in the jelly when it begins to thicken; pour into a large mould, set in ice-water in a cool place, and, when ready to serve, turn out as you would jelly, only that you have the pudding in a deep dish.

Make a sauce as for snow pudding, and pour around the pudding, or, if you prefer, serve in a separate dish. This makes a large pudding: half of it is enough for a small family.

Royal Cream.

One quart of milk, one-third of a box of gelatine four tablespoonfuls of sugar, three eggs, vanilla. Put the gelatine into the milk, and let it stand half an hour Beat the yolks well with the sugar, and stir into the milk. Set the kettle into a pan of hot water, and stir until it begins to thicken like soft custard.

Have ready the whites of the eggs beaten to a stiff froth; and, the moment you take the kettle from the fire, stir them in quickly, and turn into the moulds. Set away in a cold place to harden.

When you cannot get cream to make Charlotte Russe with, this makes a good filling, if you omit the whites and fill your moulds when the cream is perfectly cold but not yet hardened.

Red Grout.

Take currant juice, and add an equal quantity of water. Put it over the fire, and, when boiling, add four tablespoonfuls of ground rice, which has been mixed with half a cup of cold water, to one quart of the liquid. Stir carefully until it thickens, then add sugar enough to give it a good flavor. Pour into moulds, and set away to cool. To be eaten with sugar and cream the same as *blanc-mange.* If you have not the ground rice, cornstarch will do.

Cream Pudding Sauce.

One cup of powdered sugar, one egg, one-third of a cup of cream or milk. Beat the white of the egg to a stiff froth, then add the yolk and sugar, and beat well. Flavor with vanilla, lemon, or wine, and add the cream the last thing. This sauce is nice for a light pudding.

Molasses Candy.

Two cups of molasses, one of white sugar, one tablespoonful of vinegar, a small piece of butter. Boil from twenty minutes to half an hour. Try it by dropping a little into cold water: if it hardens, it is ready to cool. Pour into a flat, buttered dish, and, when cool, work it with the hands.

Peanut Candy.

Prepare the same as the above: let boil ten minutes longer; and, just before taking off the fire, add a pint of nuts, which have been shelled and broken.

Pour into the dish; and, before it becomes perfectly cold, cut into pieces.

Walnut and Hickory nut same as a[bove]

Chocolate Candy.

One cup of molasses, two of sugar, one of milk, one-half of chocolate, a piece of butter half the size of an egg.

Boil the milk and molasses together, scrape the chocolate fine, and mix with just enough of the boiling milk and molasses to moisten: rub it perfectly smooth then, with the sugar, stir into the boiling liquid, add the butter, and boil twenty minutes. Try as molasses candy; and, if it hardens, pour into a buttered dish. Cut the same as nut candy.

Vinegar Candy.

One cup of vinegar, two of white sugar. Boil until

it will break brittle when dropped in cold water. Pour into a butter-dish, and cut before it gets hard.

This is nice with nuts for a change. Any kind will answer.

To make Mead.

One pint and a half of brown sugar, half a pint of molasses. Pour on this three pints of boiling water. Let this stand until blood warm, then add two ounces of tartaric acid and one of essence of sassafras.

When cold bottle.

To use Mead.

Put one tablespoonful of the mead in the bottom of a glass, then fill two-thirds full of cold water, then stir in one-fourth of a teaspoonful of soda, and drink while foaming.

To make good Soap.

Ten pounds of potash, eleven of fat, three or four pails of boiling water. Pour on and stir until it is dissolved. After a few days add boiling water until a proper thickness.

Black-Walnut Stain.

One-fourth of a pound of asphaltum, one-half of beeswax, one gallon of turpentine. If too thin add beeswax; if too light, asphaltum. Soft pine is the wood that stains most readily and prettily.

Roast Ham.

Prepare the ham as for boiling, and if good-sized (say ten pounds) boil three hours. Take off the skin and place in a baking pan. Let it cook in a moderate oven two hours, and serve with champagne sauce.

With one tablespoonful of butter mix thoroughly one tablespoonful of flour. Set the saucepan on the fire and stir constantly until it is a dark brown, then pour into it half a pint of boiling gravy, (the liquor in which pieces of green meat have been boiling until it is very rich). Pour the gravy in slowly, and stir slowly and constantly. Let it boil up once, season well with pepper and salt, and strain. Add half a cup of champagne and serve.

Vinaigrette Sauce.

One teaspoonful of white pepper, one of salt, one-half of mustard, half a cup of vinegar, one tablespoonful of oil. Mix salt, pepper, and mustard together, then *very* slowly add the vinegar, and after all is well mixed add the oil. To be eaten on cold meats or fish.

Graham Bread.

Where the bread is liked light like the baker's, this is a good rule; but if the bread be eaten for medicinal purposes the rule in the first part of the book is the best.

Half a cup of yeast, one pint of warm milk or water, and flour enough to make a thin batter. Let this rise over night and in the morning stir in half a cup of sugar, a little salt, one teaspoonful of saleratus dissolved in water and Graham enough to make a very stiff batter. All the other ingredients should be thoroughly beaten into the sponge before adding the Graham, then stir in the Graham a little at a time, and beat well. Much depends upon the beating. Shape into loaves with the hands, and place in the baking-pans. If the weather is warm and the sponge is light the loaves will be ready to bake in an hour and a half; but if not warm it will take longer. The oven should not be so hot as for white bread. Bake one hour and a half.

Graham Muffin.—Very Nice.

Into a bowl put one and a half pints of Graham, half a cup of sugar, and a little salt. Now into the seive put half a pint of flour, one teaspoonful of saleratus and two of cream tartar. Mix thoroughly with the flour, and then sift on to the material in the bowl. Mix all the ingredients thoroughly while dry, and then add two well beaten eggs and milk enough to make a batter that will drop from the spoon readily. Fill the muffin-cups about two-thirds full, and bake in a quick oven.

Rye-Muffins.

Made the same as Graham.

Sponge Drops.

Make cake the same as the first rule for sponge cake on page 91. Have the muffin cups very lightly larded, and drop a teaspoonful of the mixture into each cup. Bake in a quick oven. These are very nice for a desert or for tea.

Brandied Peaches.

Weigh your peaches, then throw them a few at a time into boiling lye. As soon as the skin begins to curl up, drain them and rub the skin smoothly off with a cloth, then throw them into cold water. After you have finished put them over the fire in boiling water, but do not let them boil. When they are soft enough to make a dent in them, take them out to cool. Cover them with white brandy, and let them stand twenty-four hours, then make a syrup of a pound of sugar to a pound of peaches, and mix them. Cover them close, and in a few days they will be ready for use.

Sour-Orange Preserve.

Grate off the rind and cut the orange into two parts, take out all the pulp. Weigh them and place in a large stone pot and cover with a brine made from three gallons of water and one quart of salt. Let them stand in this twenty-four hours and then drain off the brine. Cover again with a brine made with the same amount of water and half as much salt as in the first Let them stand twenty-four hours again. Now drain again, and cover with clear cold water and let them stand in this twenty-four hours. Drain again and put into a boiler and cover with cold water; let them come to a boil and then boil fifteen minutes; take them out and drain. Make a syrup of sugar (pound for pound), and water enough to dissolve. When the syrup is clear, drop in the oranges and boil until they are clear and tender, which will be in about four hours of slow boiling. Great care must be taken that they do not scorch. They must be stirred every ten or fifteen minutes. The sugar may be either white or brown. The orange used is not the common market orange, but the wild, sour orange found in Florida.

Pickled Blueberries.

Nearly fill a jar with ripe berries, and then fill up with good molasses, cover, and set away, and in a few weeks they will be ready for use.

To Blanch Almonds.

Shell the nuts and pour *boiling* water over them, let them stand in the boiling water a minute, and then throw them into *cold* water. Rub between the hands, and the dark skin will come off readily.

To Sweeten Tainted Meat.

Cover the meat with sweet milk, and let it stand an hour or two, and, unless the meat is very bad, it will make it perfectly sweet. Soaking in saleratus water is also good.

To Cleanse New Stove Furniture.

Boil skim-milk in the pots, kettles, pans, &c., and then wash in good soap-suds.

To Restore Color to Furniture, etc.

When the color has been taken out of any thing, that is painted, by alcohol, rub the place briskly with a piece of flannel and kerosene, and, in a few minutes, it will turn dark again.

Marking Cakes in Gold.

Bake small round cakes for the children, and, when the frosting is hard on them, dip a small brush in the yolk of egg, and write the child's name on the cake. It pleases the little ones very much to see their names in this way.

Chocolate Caramel.

Three pounds brown sugar, coarse, one-half pound of butter, one-half pound of chocolate scraped fine, one pint cream or milk. Melt all these together with care, and boil twenty minutes or half an hour, stirring all the time. Just before taking it off the fire, pour in vanilla to flavor, and stir in half or a whole cup of granulated sugar. Pour it in a pan, and, when half cool, score it. It should be half an inch thick, and be cut up into pieces about an inch square.

Molasses Candy.

Two cups of sugar, one of molasses, one-half of butter, one-fourth of vinegar, vanilla and peanuts. Boil until it will candy, then stir in vanilla and peanuts, and pour into a pan. Score the same as caramel.

Vinegar Candy.

Two cups of molasses, two tablespoonfuls of sugar, two of vinegar.

Chocolate Cream.

Two cups of powdered sugar, nearly a cup of water. Boil about five minutes, then beat until it turns to a cream, after which make into drops, and dip them into the melted chocolate. Melt three-fourths of a cake of chocolate by scraping into a bowl, and then placing the bowl either over the teakettle or into a pan of hot water.

Molasses Candy.

Two cups of molasses, one of sugar, butter the size of an egg, one tablespoonful of checkerberry. Pull when done.

www.ingramcontent.com/pod-product-compliance
Lightning Source LLC
Chambersburg PA
CBHW021802230426
43669CB00008B/602